G. SCHIRMER'S
COLLECTION OF
OPERA LIBRETTOS

TRISTAN UND ISOLDE

Opera in Three Acts

by

Richard Wagner

English Version by
STEWART ROBB

ED. 2673

G. SCHIRMER, *Inc.*

Important Notice

Performances of this opera must be licensed by the publisher.

All rights of any kind with respect to this opera and any parts thereof, including but not limited to stage, radio, television, motion picture, mechanical reproduction, translation, printing, and selling are strictly reserved.

License to perform this work, in whole or in part, whether with instrumental or keyboard accompaniment, must be secured in writing from the Publisher. Terms will be quoted upon request.

Copying of either separate parts or the whole of this work, by hand or by any other process, is unlawful and punishable under the provisions of the U.S.A. Copyright Act.

The use of any copies, including arrangements and orchestrations, other than those issued by the Publisher, is forbidden.

All inquiries should be directed to the Publisher:

G. Schirmer Rental Department
5 Bellvale Road
Chester, NY 10918
(914) 469-2271

TRISTAN UND ISOLDE

In his stormy personal life, Richard Wagner remains the prototype of the late-romantic artist. Indeed, his *Tristan und Isolde* was inspired in part by the composer's romantic attachment to the poetess Mathilde Wesendonk, the beautiful wife of a silk merchant in Zurich who assisted Wagner during one of his recurring financial crises by giving him room, board and cash. During the courtship, Wagner set five of Mme. Wesendonk's verses to music, two of which — *Träume* and *Im Treibhaus* — he later used as leitmotifs for 'Tristan's love music and the prelude to Act III. Perhaps the sense of unfulfilled desire that permeates the score of Tristan derives in part from the composer's own anguish of that time.

More important to *Tristan und Isolde,* however, was Wagner's revolutionary feeling about the musical theater, its style and dramatic form. He sought to create a new art form — not opera — in which words, music and action would become indivisibly one. He termed the form *Gesamtkunstwerk:* total art work. To compose *Tristan,* which in dramatic conciseness is the most perfect example of his concept, Wagner had to put aside work on a much larger project, the *Ring* tetralogy. With *Tristan* he planned to turn out a more practical work, one that could be easily produced, employing a small cast and an almost Spartan story line.

The idea for a music drama on the Tristan legend had come to Wagner as early as 1854, but he did not begin the score until 1857. (He completed the manuscript on April 8, 1859, while living in Lucern.) As usual Wagner wrote his own text, retelling the story of the Cornish knight first chronicled in an ancient Celtic romance set down during the twelfth century by Thomas of Britain. He was aided by a German version of his tale adapted by Gottfried von Strassburg in 1220.

In *Tristan und Isolde* Wagner unleashed an entire new vocabulary of harmony which has determined the course of music ever since. He literally revolutionized opera by placing the singers at the service of the drama and so elaborating the orchestral texture that each act became a symphonic poem in itself. His daring expansion of the borders of tonality, his use of restless, yearning chromatic suspensions and unresolved chord progressions, caused many of his musical contemporaries to judge him mad. But it was not long before the world came to understand what he was striving to achieve, and the twelve-tone system of composition developed early in the twentieth century by Arnold Schoenberg could not have been conceived except on the basis of *Tristan,* a milestone in world art.

The world premiere of *Tristan und Isolde* took place at the National Theater in Munich on June 10, 1865. Schnorr von Carolsfeld and his wife sang the title roles, and despite their celebrity, the work had to be dropped from the repertory after three performances, so cold was the critical and public reception. Only the intervention of Wagner's patron, King Ludwig of Bavaria, prevented it from being cancelled after the first performance. A projected earlier production in Vienna was abandoned after fifty-seven rehearsals when the singers and orchestra insisted the music was both unsingable and unplayable!

Tristan und Isolde, nevertheless, made its way. The American premiere at the Metropolitan Opera House on December 1, 1886 proved an outstanding success. With Wagner's close friend Anton Seidl conducting, the production featured Lilli Lehmann (Isolde), Albert Niemann (Tristan), Marianne Brant (Brangaene), Adolf Robinson (Kurvenal) and Emil Fischer (King Mark). After that the work was given in the old Metropolitan Opera House on 293 other occasions. Among the most memorable performances there were those with Lillian Nordica and Jean de Reszke during the 1890's; those with Olive Fremstad about 1910, with either Gustav Mahler or Arturo Toscanini conducting; and those that starred the team of Kirsten Flagstad and Lauritz Melchior, Artur Bodanzsky at the helm, during the late 1930's. In recent seasons an outstanding Isolde was the Swedish soprano Brigit Nilsson, who made her New York debut in the part on December 18, 1959.

THE STORY

ACT I. Against her will, the proud Irish princess Isolde is being conducted by the knight Tristan over the seas to the court of his uncle, King Mark of Cornwall, whom she is to marry. Taunted by the songs of a sailor, she rails at her captor and, through her maid Brangaene, bids him come forward and face her wrath. When Tristan declines, Isolde tells Brangaene how, long before, he had fought with the Irish knight Morold, who had gone to Cornwall to collect the tribute due to Ireland, and to whom Isolde had been engaged. Morold had been killed, Isolde continues, and Tristan injured, and she relates how she made the mistake of nursing the knight back to health in Ireland instead of slaying him in vengeance. Recalling how Tristan repaid her tenderness by returning to claim her for his uncle, she concludes with a curse upon his head. Overwhelmed by shame and bitterness, the princess decides to drink a death potion, which she bids her maid prepare from a magic store bequeathed her by her mother. Tristan enters when the shouts of the sailors reveal that the ship is nearing land. Calling on him to atone for the murder of Morold, Isolde refuses to put him to death by the sword, as he suggests, but bids him drink the death potion with her. Meanwhile the horrified Brangaene has substituted a love philter in the cup that Tristan and Isolde now raise to their lips. After a pause they are overcome by the magic and yield to the passion that had hitherto been stifled. Aghast at what she has done, Brangaene rushes to separate the lovers as the ship approaches Cornwall, where they are greeted by King Mark's court.

ACT II. In the castle garden, Isolde hears the horns of the king's hunting party recede into the twilight and tells Brangaene to signal Tristan that it is safe for him to enter. The princess absolves the maid of responsibilty for her act, bidding her now to keep watch for Mark's return. Tristan rushes in; the lovers exchange passionate declarations as they invoke the longed-for night to descend upon them. Lost in each other's embrace, they ignore Brangaene's repeated warnings that the hours are flying and so are surprised by the king, who appears with his party and halts in consternation. There is a long pause; day begins to dawn. At last Mark sorrowfully berates Tristan for his treachery, calling upon all to see how the truest of the true has proved false. Tristan, offering no defense, tenderly invites Isolde to share his dark future and, when she agrees, kisses her gently on the forehead. Mark's knight Melot draws his sword in fury and advances on Tristan, who drops his guard and allows himself to be wounded.

ACT III. Tristan awaits Isolde in his ruined castle of Kareol in Brittany, where a shepherd pipes mournfully to indicate that no ship can be seen. Lying on a couch, the knight wakes from a fevered sleep and turns to Kurvenal, the faithful servant who has brought him from Cornwall to recuperate from his wound. In his delirium Tristan assures Kurvenal of Isolde's return, painting a vivid picture of the ship that will bring her to him. After a while the shepherd's pipe is heard playing merrily. Beside himself with joy, the knight listens as his servant describes the actual ship's arrival, and when Isolde is sighted he wildly tears the bandage from his wound. She rushes in and Tristan dies in her arms. Mark and Melot, who have pursued Isolde, burst upon the scene and are engaged in battle by the grief-stricken Kurvenal, who slays Melot and in turn is mortally wounded by the king's defenders. The senseless Isolde is revived by Brangaene, who reveals that she has told Mark of the love potion and that he has come not to punish but to forgive. But the magnanimous king is too late. Isolde, gazing with rapture upon Tristan's face, breathes a final invocation and then sinks, lifeless and transfigured, upon his body.

Courtesy of Opera News

CAST OF CHARACTERS

TRISTAN . . . . Tenor

KING MARK . . . . Bass

ISOLDE . . . . Soprano

KURVENAL . . . . Baritone

MELOT . . . . Tenor

BRANGAENE . . . . Soprano

A SHEPHERD . . . . Tenor

A HELMSMAN . . . . Baritone

Sailors, Knights, Attendants

SYNOPSIS OF SCENES

TRISTAN UND ISOLDE

ERSTER AUFZUG

*Zeltartiges Gemach auf dem Vorderdeck
eines Seeschiffes, reich mit Teppichen
behangen, beim Beginn nach dem Hintergrunde zu gänzlich geschlossen; zur
Seite führt eine schmale Treppe in den
Schiffsraum hinab.*

*Isolde auf einem Ruhebett, das Gesicht in
die Kissen gedrückt. Brangäne, einen
Teppich zurückgeschlagen haltend, blickt
zur Seite über Bord.*

ERSTER AUFTRITT

STIMME EINES JUNGEN SEEMANNS
*(aus der Höhe, wie von
Mast her, vernehmbar)*

Westwärts
schweift der Blick:
ostwärts
streicht das Schiff.
Frisch weht der Wind
der Heimat zu:
mein irisch Kind,
wo weilest du?
Sind's deiner Seufzer Wehen,
die mir die Segel blähen?
Wehe, wehe, du Wind!
Weh, ach wehe, mein Kind!
Irische Maid,
du wilde, minnige Maid!

ISOLDE *(jäh auffahrend)*

Wer wagt mich zu höhnen?
(Sie blickt verstört um sich.)
Brangäne, du?
Sag — wo sind wir?

BRANGÄNE *(an der Öffnung)*

Blaue Streifen
stiegen im Westen auf;
sanft und schnell
segelt das Schiff:
auf ruhiger See vor Abend
erreichen wir sicher das Land.

ISOLDE

Welches Land?

BRANGÄNE

Kornwalls grünen Strand.

ISOLDE

Nimmermehr!
Nicht heut noch morgen!

BRANGÄNE
*(läßt den Vorhang zufallen und
eilt bestürzt zu Isolde)*

Was hör' ich? Herrin! Ha!

ISOLDE *(wild, vor sich hin)*

Entartet Geschlecht!
Unwert der Ahnen!
Wohin, Mutter,
vergabst du die Macht,
über Meer und Sturm zu gebieten?
O zahme Kunst
der Zauberin,
die nur Balsamtränke noch braut!
Erwache mir wieder,
kühne Gewalt;
herauf aus dem Busen,
wo du dich bargst!
Hört meinen Willen,
zagende Winde!
Heran zu Kampf
und Wettergetös'!
Zu tobender Stürme
wütendem Wirbel!
Treibt aus dem Schlaf
dies träumende Meer,
weckt aus dem Grund
seine grollende Gier!
Zeigt ihm die Beute,
die ich ihm biete!
Zerschlag es dies trotzige Schiff,
des zerschellten Trümmer verschling's!
Und was auf ihm lebt,
den wehenden Atem,
den laß ich euch Winden zum Lohn!

1

TRISTAN AND ISOLDE

ACT I

A pavilion, richly hung with rugs, on the forward deck of a sailing ship, at first entirely closed at the back; on one side a narrow hatchway leads to the cabin below.

Isolde on a couch, her face buried in the cushions. Brangaene, her maidservant, holding back a curtain, looks out over the side of the ship.

Scene I

THE VOICE OF A YOUNG SAILOR
(from above, as if from the masthead)

Westward
roams my gaze:
eastward
plies the ship.
The wind blows fresh
toward land of home:
my Irish child,
where do you roam?
Is it your windy sighing
that keeps my vessel flying?
Breezes, blow; breezes, blow!
Child, they bring only woe!
My Irish maid,
you wild, lovable maid!

ISOLDE
(starting up, and looking around, disturbed)

Who here dares to mock me?
Brangaene, ho!
Say—where are we?

BRANGAENE *(at the opening)*

Blue the streaks
that rise from the western sky;
soft and swift,
onward we sail;
a sea that is calm will bring us
quite safely to land ere it's dark.

ISOLDE

What land?

BRANGAENE

Cornwall's grassy shore.

ISOLDE

Nevermore,
today or ever!

BRANGAENE
(lets fall the curtain and hastens anxiously to Isolde)

What say you? Mistress! Ha!

ISOLDE *(with wild gaze)*

Degenerate stock!
Shame of your forebears!
Where now, Mother,
have you given your power
to command the sea and the tempest?
O feeble art
of sorceress,
that now only brews balsam drink!
Bold spirit of mast'ry,
rouse me again;
come out from that bosom
wherein you hide!
Hear, trembling winds,
the orders I give you!
To arms, to breast
the elements' roar
and blustering tempest's
furious vortex!
Drive from its sleep
this slumbering sea,
stir up the deep
till it growls in its greed!
Show it the booty
which I now offer!
Demolish this insolent ship,
let it break and shiver to bits!
And all that survives,
as flickering spirits,
I leave to you winds for your pay!

1

BRANGÄNE
(im äußersten Schreck, um Isolde
sich bemühend)
O weh!
Ach! Ach
des Übels, das ich geahnt!
Isolde! Herrin!
Teures Herz!
Was bargst du mir so lang?
Nicht eine Träne
weintest du Vater und Mutter;
kaum einen Gruß
den Bleibenden botest du.
Von der Heimat scheidend
kalt und stumm,
bleich und schweigend
auf der Fahrt;
ohne Nahrung,
ohne Schlaf;
starr und elend,
wild verstört:
wie ertrug ich,
so dich sehend,
nichts dir mehr zu sein,
fremd vor dir zu stehn?
O, nun melde,
was dich müht!
Sage, künde,
was dich quält!
Herrin Isolde,
trauteste Holde!
Soll sie wert sich dir wähnen,
vertraue nun Brangänen!

ISOLDE
Luft! Luft!
Mir erstickt das Herz!
Öffne! Öffne dort weit!
(Brangäne zieht eilig die Vorhänge in der
Mitte auseinander.)

ZWEITER AUFTRITT
Man blickt dem Schiff entlang bis zum
Steuerbord, über den Bord hinaus auf
das Meer und den Horizont. Um den
Hauptmast in der Mitte ist Seevolk, mit
Tauen beschäftigt, gelagert; über sie hin-
aus gewahrt man am Steuerbord Ritter
und Knappen, ebenfalls gelagert; von
ihnen etwas entfernt Tristan, mit ver-
schränkten Armen stehend und sinnend
in das Meer blickend; zu Füßen ihm,
nachlässig gelagert, Kurwenal.

STIMME DES JUNGEN SEEMANNS
Frisch weht der Wind
der Heimat zu:

mein irisch Kind,
wo weilest du?
Sind's deiner Seufzer Wehen,
die mir die Segel blähen?
Wehe, wehe, du Wind!
Weh, ach wehe, mein Kind!

ISOLDE
(deren Blick sogleich Tristan fand und starr
auf ihn geheftet blieb, dumpf für sich)
Mir erkoren,
mir verloren,
hehr und heil,
kühn und feig!
Todgeweihtes Haupt!
Todgeweihtes Herz!
(Zu Brangäne, unheimlich lachend.)
Was hältst du von dem Knechte?

BRANGÄNE *(ihrem Blicke folgend)*
Wen meinst du?

ISOLDE
Dort den Helden,
der meinem Blick
den seinen birgt,
in Scham und Scheue
abwärts schaut.
Sag, wie dünkt er dich?

BRANGÄNE
Frägst du nach Tristan,
teure Frau,
dem Wunder aller Reiche,
dem hochgepriesnen Mann,
dem Helden ohne Gleiche,
des Ruhmes Hort und Bann?

ISOLDE *(sie verhöhnend)*
Der zagend vor dem Streiche
sich flüchtet, wo er kann,
weil eine Braut er als Leiche
für seinen Herrn gewann!
Dünkt es dich dunkel,
mein Gedicht?
Frag ihn denn selbst,
den freien Mann,
ob mir zu nahn er wagt?
Der Ehren Gruß
und zücht'ge Acht
vergißt der Herrin
der zage Held,
daß ihr Blick ihn nur nicht erreiche,
den Helden ohne Gleiche!
O, er weiß
wohl, warum!
Zu dem Stolzen geh,
meld ihm der Herrin Wort:
Meinem Dienst bereit,
schleunig soll er mir nahn.

BRANGAENE
(in alarm and concern for Isolde)

O woe!
Ah! Ah!
The ill I feared has arrived!
Isolde! Mistress!
Dearest heart!
What have you hid so long?
You did not shed
one tear for your father and mother;
you scarcely bade
farewell to those left behind,
and with stony coldness
left your home,
pale and silent
all the trip;
food you took not,
nor did sleep,
numb and wretched,
wild, distraught:
how could I endure
to see this?
Am I nothing now,
nothing but a stone?
Just what was it
tired you so?
Tell me plainly
what torments.
Lady Isolde,
dearly beloved one,
if you think she is worthy,
then you should trust Brangaene.

ISOLDE

Air! Air!
Oh, my heart constricts!
Open, open there wide!

(Brangaene hastily draws apart the curtains in the center.)

SCENE II

One can see the whole length of the ship to starboard, with the sea and the horizon beyond. In the center, above the mainmast, are sailors, busied with ropes, and lying around; beyond them, in the stern, are groups of knights and attendants, also seated; a little apart stands Tristan, his arms folded, gazing thoughtfully out to sea; at his feet Kurvenal reclines carelessly. From the masthead above is once more heard the voice of the young sailor.

THE VOICE OF THE YOUNG SAILOR

The wind blows fresh
toward land of home:

my Irish child,
where do you roam?
Is it your windy sighing
that keeps my vessel flying?
Breezes, blow; breezes, blow!
Child, they bring only woe!

ISOLDE
(whose eyes have at once sought Tristan and fixed stonily on him—aside, gloomily)

My elected,
now the lost one,
great and strong,
brave and craven!
Death-devoted head!
Death-devoted heart!
(To Brangaene, laughing unnaturally.)
What think you of that fellow?

BRANGAENE *(following her look)*
Whom mean you?

ISOLDE

There, the hero,
who cannot look me
in the eye,
but looks away
in frightened shame.
Say, what d'you think of him?

BRANGAENE

Can you mean Tristan,
lady dear,   .
that marvel of all nations,
that pinnacle of praise,
that hero without equal,
the prize and vaunt of fame?

ISOLDE *(scornfully)*
Who, trembling at his triumph,
seeks refuge where he can,
fearing to bring to his sov'reign
a corpse instead of a bride.
Think you my saying
is too dark?
Ask him yourself,
that free-born man,
if he will dare come near.
The shrinking hero
has forgot
the forms of greeting
and respect,
for he fears that her glance may reach him,
this hero without equal!
Oh, he knows
well, just why!
To this proud one, go,
bear him his lady's word!
Let him straightway come,
ready for my command.

BRANGÄNE

Soll ich ihn bitten,
dich zu grüßen?

ISOLDE

Befehlen ließ
dem Eigenholde
Furcht der Herrin
ich, Isolde!
(*Auf Isoldes gebieterischen Wink entfernt sich Brangäne und schreitet verschämt dem Deck entlang dem Steuerbord zu, an den arbeitenden Seeleuten vorbei. Isolde, mit starrem Blicke ihr folgend, zieht sich rücklings nach dem Ruhebett zurück, wo sie sitzend während des Folgenden bleibt, das Auge unabgewandt nach dem Steuerbord gerichtet.*)

KURWENAL

(*der Brangäne kommen sieht, zupft, ohne sich zu erheben, Tristan am Gewande*)

Hab acht, Tristan!
Botschaft von Isolde.

TRISTAN (*auffahrend*)

Was ist? Isolde? —
(*Er faßt sich schnell, als Brangäne vor ihm anlangt und sich verneigt.*)
Von meiner Herrin?
Ihr gehorsam
was zu hören
meldet höfisch
mir die traute Magd?

BRANGÄNE

Mein Herre Tristan,
Euch zu sehen
wünscht Isolde,
meine Frau.

TRISTAN

Grämt sie die lange Fahrt,
die geht zu End';
eh noch die Sonne sinkt,
sind wir am Land.
Was meine Frau mir befehle,
treulich sei's erfüllt.

BRANGÄNE

So mög' Herr Tristan
zu ihr gehn:
das ist der Herrin Will'.

TRISTAN

Wo dort die grünen Fluren
dem Blick noch blau sich färben,
harrt mein König
meiner Frau:
zu ihm sie zu geleiten,
bald nah' ich mich der Lichten;

keinem gönnt' ich
diese Gunst.

BRANGÄNE

Mein Herre Tristan,
höre wohl:
deine Dienste
will die Frau,
daß du zur Stell' ihr nahtest
dort, wo sie deiner harrt.

TRISTAN

Auf jeder Stelle,
wo ich steh',
getreulich dien' ich ihr,
der Frauen höchster Ehr';
ließ' ich das Steuer
jetzt zur Stund',
wie lenkt' ich sicher den Kiel
zu König Markes Land?

BRANGÄNE

Tristan, mein Herre!
Was höhnst du mich?
Dünkt dich nicht deutlich
die tör'ge Magd,
hör meiner Herrin Wort!
So, hieß sie, sollt' ich sagen:
Befehlen ließ'
dem Eigenholde
Furcht der Herrin
sie, Isolde.

KURWENAL (*aufspringend*)

Darf ich die Antwort sagen?

TRISTAN (*ruhig*)

Was wohl erwidertest du?

KURWENAL

Das sage sie
der Frau Isold'!
Wer Kornwalls Kron'
und Englands Erb'
an Irlands Maid vermacht,
der kann der Magd
nicht eigen sein,
die selbst dem Ohm er schenkt.
Ein Herr der Welt
Tristan der Held!
Ich ruf's: du sag's, und grollten
mir tausend Frau Isolden!

(*Da Tristan durch Gebärden ihm zu wehren sucht und Brangäne entrüstet sich zum Weggehen wendet, singt Kurwenal der zögernd sich Entfernenden mit höchster Stärke nach:*)

„Herr Morold zog
zu Meere her,
in Kornwall Zins zu haben;

BRANGAENE

Am I to bid him
offer duty?

ISOLDE

Just let this lord,
so self-sufficient,
fear his mistress,
me, Isolde!

(*At a gesture of command from Isolde, Brangaene leaves her, and timidly makes her way along the deck, past the busy sailors, to the stern; Isolde gazes after with a blank expression, then sinks back on the couch, where she remains seated during the following, her eyes still fixed sternward.*)

KURVENAL

(*sees Brangaene coming, and plucks Tristan by the robe without rising*)

Beware, Tristan!
Message from Isolde.

TRISTAN (*starting*)

What's that? Isolde?

(*He quickly masters himself as Brangaene approaches and curtsies.*)

You're from my lady?
Does she give you
courtly orders
brought this servant
by her faithful maid?

BRANGAENE

My lord, Sir Tristan,
Dame Isolde
wishes you to
come to her.

TRISTAN

Her journey must seem long
but soon will end.
Before the sun has set
we'll be ashore.
Let but my lady command me:
straight it shall be done.

BRANGAENE

Let then Lord Tristan
go to her:
that is the lady's will.

TRISTAN

There, where the grassy meadows
to sight look blue in color,
there my master
waits my dame:
I soon must see the Bright One
and lead her to my sov'reign;

there's no other
favored so.

BRANGAENE

My master Tristan,
listen well:
since your service
is required,
my mistress asks your presence
there where she waits for you.

TRISTAN

I give my duty
where I stand,
in service ever true
to her of crowning name.
If I this instant
left the helm,
how could I safely direct
the ship to King Mark's land?

BRANGAENE

Tristan, my master!
Why mock at me?
If words are cloudy
from foolish maid,
hark to my lady's words.
Thus, said she, should I tell you:
"Just let this lord
so self-sufficient,
fear his mistress,
me, Isolde!"

KURVENAL (*springing up*)

Dare I supply the answer?

TRISTAN (*calmly*)

What kind of answer have you?

KURVENAL

This let her say
to Dame Isolde:
If Cornwall's crown
and England's fee
to Ireland's maid are made,
he cannot be
the chattel of
the prize he brings his lord.
A lord world-famed,
Tristan the great!
I've said: despite complaining
from a thousand Dame Isoldes.

While Tristan by gestures tries to silence him, and Brangaene, offended, turns to go away, Kurvenal, as she slowly moves away, sings after her at the top of his voice.

"Lord Morold crossed
the wat'ry wave,
for Cornish tax he harried;

ein Eiland schwimmt
auf ödem Meer,
da liegt er nun begraben!
Sein Haupt doch hängt
im Irenland,
als Zins gezahlt
von Engeland:
Hei! Unser Held Tristan,
wie der Zins zahlen kann!"

*(Kurwenal, von Tristan fortgescholten, ist in
den Schiffsraum hinabgestiegen; Brangäne
in Bestürzung zu Isolde zurückgekehrt,
schließt hinter sich die Vorhänge, während
die ganze Mannschaft außen sich hören
läßt.)*

ALLE MÄNNER
Sein Haupt doch hängt
im Irenland,
als Zins gezahlt
von Engeland:
Hei! Unser Held Tristan,
wie der Zins zahlen kann!

DRITTER AUFTRITT
*Isolde und Brangäne allein, bei vollkom-
men wieder geschlossenen Vorhängen.
Isolde erhebt sich mit verzweiflungsvoller
Wutgebärde. Brangäne stürtzt ihr zu Fü-
ßen.*

BRANGÄNE
Weh, ach wehe!
Dies zu dulden!

ISOLDE
*(dem furchtbarsten Ausbruche nahe,
schnell sich zusammenraffend)*
Doch nun von Tristan!
Genau will ich's vernehmen.

BRANGÄNE
Ach, frage nicht!

ISOLDE
Frei sag's ohne Furcht!

BRANGÄNE
Mit höf'schen Worten
wich er aus.

ISOLDE
Doch als du deutlich mahntest?

BRANGÄNE
Da ich zur Stell'
ihn zu dir rief:
wo er auch steh',

so sagte er,
getreulich dien' er ihr,
der Frauen höchster Ehr';
ließ' er das Steuer
jetzt zur Stund',
wie lenkt' er sicher den Kiel
zu König Markes Land?

ISOLDE *(schmerzlich bitter)*
„Wie lenkt' er sicher den Kiel
zu König Markes Land?" *(Grell und heftig.)*
Den Zins ihm auszuzahlen,
den er aus Irland zog!

BRANGÄNE
Auf deine eignen Worte,
als ich ihm die entbot,
ließ seinen Treuen Kurwenal —

ISOLDE
Den hab' ich wohl vernommen,
kein Wort, was mir entging.
Erfuhrest du meine Schmach,
nun höre, was sie mir schuf.
Wie lachend sie
mir Lieder singen,
wohl könnt' auch ich erwidern
von einem Kahn,
der klein und arm
an Irlands Küste schwamm,
darinnen krank
ein siecher Mann
elend im Sterben lag.
Isolde Kunst
ward ihm bekannt;
mit Heilsalben
und Balsamsaft
der Wunde, die ihn plagte,
getreulich pflag sie da.
Der „Tantris"
mit sorgender List sich nannte,
als Tristan
Isold' ihn bald erkannte,
da in des Müß'gen Schwerte
eine Scharte sie gewahrte,
darin genau
sich fügt' ein Splitter,
den einst im Haupt
des Iren-Ritter,
zum Hohn ihr heimgesandt,
mit kund'ger Hand sie fand.
Da schrie's mir auf
aus tiefstem Grund!
Mit dem hellen Schwert
ich vor ihm stund,
an ihm, dem Überfrechen,
Herrn Morolds Tod zu rächen.
Von seinem Lager
blickt' er her —

a lonely island
holds his grave,
where he lies now quite buried!
His head now hangs
in Irish land,
the tax returned
by Engeland:
Here's to our lord Tristan,
for the tax, what a man!"

*Kurvenal, driven away by Tristan, goes be-
low to the cabin; Brangaene, much disturbed,
returns to Isolde, and closes the curtains behind her while the whole crew is heard
singing without.*

ALL THE MEN

"His head now hangs
in Irish land,
the tax returned
by Engeland:
Here's to our lord Tristan,
for the tax, what a man!"

SCENE III

*Isolde and Brangaene alone; the curtains
are again completely closed. Isolde rises
with a despairing gesture of wrath. Brangaene falls at her feet.*

BRANGAENE

Woe! What sorrow
must be suffered!

ISOLDE

(restraining herself from a furious outbreak)

What now of Tristan?
I wish to know exactly.

BRANGAENE

Ah, do not ask!

ISOLDE

Speak out without fear.

BRANGAENE

His courtly phrases
told no tale.

ISOLDE

But when you plainly asked him?

BRANGAENE

When I had plainly
bid him come:
just where he stands,

he said to me,
he truly serves you well,
this pearl of womanhood;
if he this instant
left the helm,
how could he safely direct
the boat to King Mark's land?

ISOLDE *(bitterly)*

"How could he safely direct
the boat to King Mark's land?"
To pay the tax again
that he brings from Ireland's realm!

BRANGAENE

When I announced your message
and in your very words,
then did his servant Kurvenal . . .

ISOLDE

That did I hear quite clearly;
I did not miss a word.
My maid has witnessed my shame;
now listen how it was wrought.
They sing derisive
songs against me.
Yet I could well requite them:
about a boat
both small and mean
that sailed to Ireland's coast;
and there, within,
a man lay sick,
wretched, at point of death.
Isolde's skill
became his help.
Her salves soothed him,
and healing balms;
the wounds from which he suffered
she tended faithfully.
Most slyly
he went by the name of "Tantris,"
but soon Isold'
knew the man as Tristan,
when in his idle weapon
she observed a nick that marred it,
in which a splinter
fit exactly,
that in the head
of Ireland's hero,
sent home to her in scorn,
she'd found with cunning hand.
Then came a cry
from deep within!
Facing him I stood
with that bright sword,
to slay the overbold one,
and venge the death of Morold.
Then from his pallet
Tristan looked,

nicht auf das Schwert,
nicht auf die Hand —
er sah mir in die Augen.
Seines Elendes
jammerte mich! —
Das Schwert — ich ließ es fallen!
Die Morold schlug, die Wunde,
sie heilt' ich, daß er gesunde
und heim nach Hause kehre —
mit dem Blick mich nicht mehr beschwere!

BRANGÄNE

O Wunder! Wo hatt' ich die Augen?
Der Gast, den einst
ich pflegen half?

ISOLDE

Sein Lob hörest du eben:
„Hei! Unser Held Tristan" —
der war jener traur'ge Mann.
Er schwur mit tausend Eiden
mir ew'gen Dank und Treue!
Nun hör, wie ein Held
Eide hält!
Den als Tantris
unerkannt ich entlassen,
als Tristan
kehrt' er kühn zurück;
auf stolzem Schiff,
von hohem Bord,
Irlands Erbin
begehrt' er zur Eh'
für Kornwalls müden König,
für Marke, seinen Ohm.
Da Morold lebte,
wer hätt' es gewagt
uns je solche Schmach zu bieten?
Für der zinspflicht'gen
Kornen Fürsten
um Irlands Krone zu werben!
Ach, wehe mir!
Ich ja war's,
die heimlich selbst
die Schmach sich schuf!
Das rächende Schwert,
statt es zu schwingen,
machtlos ließ ich's fallen!
Nun dien' ich dem Vasallen!

BRANGÄNE

Da Friede, Sühn' und Freundschaft
von allen ward beschworen,
wir freuten uns all' des Tags;
wie ahnte mir da,
daß dir es Kummer schüf'?

ISOLDE

O blinde Augen!
Blöde Herzen!

Zahmer Mut,
verzagtes Schweigen!
Wie anders prahlte
Tristan aus,
was ich verschlossen hielt!
Die schweigend ihm
das Leben gab,
vor Feindes Rache
ihn schweigend barg;
was stumm ihr Schutz
zum Heil ihm schuf —
mit ihr gab er es preis!
Wie siegprangend
heil und hehr,
laut und hell
wies er auf mich:
„Das wär' ein Schatz,
mein Herr und Ohm;
wie dünkt Euch die zur Eh'?
Die schmucke Irin
hol' ich her;
mit Steg' und Wegen
wohlbekannt,
ein Wink, ich flieg'
nach Irenland:
Isolde, die ist Euer! —
Mir lacht das Abenteuer!"
Fluch dir, Verruchter!
Fluch deinem Haupt!
Rache! Tod!
Tod uns beiden!

BRANGÄNE

(mit ungestümer Zärtlichkeit
auf Isolde stürzend)

O Süße! Traute!
Teure! Holde!
Goldne Herrin!
Lieb' Isolde!
(Sie zieht Isolde allmählich nach dem
Ruhebett.)
Hör mich! Komme!
Setz dich her!
Welcher Wahn!
Welch eitles Zürnen!
Wie magst du dich betören,
nicht hell zu sehn noch hören?
Was je Herr Tristan
dir verdankte,
sag, konnt' er's höher lohnen
als mit der herrlichsten der Kronen?
So dient' er treu
dem edlen Ohm;
dir gab er der Welt
begehrlichsten Lohn:
dem eignen Erbe,
echt und edel,
entsagt' er zu deinen Füßen,

not on the sword,
nor at my hand,—
his eyes met mine directly;
and his misery
troubled my heart.
The sword—my hand just dropped it.
The wound he had from Morold,
I healed it, that, well in body,
he'd seek his home and leave me,
and with glances no more disturb me.

BRANGAENE

A wonder! Till now was I blinded?
The guest whom once
I helped to tend?

ISOLDE

Just now you heard his praises:
"Hail to the brave Tristan"—
he was that poor, wretched man.
A thousand oaths he swore me
of endless thanks and homage!
Now hear how a knight
holds his oath!
Who as Tantris,
unbeknown, gets his freedom,
as Tristan
boldly came again.
His ship was proud,
with lofty deck,
and he sought
Ireland's heiress as bride
for Cornwall's weary monarch,—
his uncle, who is Mark.
With Morold living,
whoever would dare
to make such affront upon us?
For that taxpaying
Cornish king
thinks to win Ireland's crown as suitor.
Ah, woe is me!
I it was
myself who wrought
my secret shame!
The sword of revenge
would not be wielded;
weakly I just dropped it.
So now I serve my vassal.

BRANGAENE

When concord, peace, and friendship
were sworn by all the parties,
that day did we all rejoice;
how could I suspect
the pain that it would cause?

ISOLDE

O eyes that see not!
Hearts so timid!

Spirit tamed,
despairing silence!
Quite otherwise he
prattled forth
what I had never breathed.
The one whose silence
spared his life,
who kept him safely
from vengeful foes;
The silent shelter
owed to her—
with her—he dared betray!
How, vic'try-flushed,
hale, sublime,
strong, he
indicated me:
"A treasure, sure,
my lord and uncle;
how does she suit as bride?
I'll fetch the pretty
Irish lass;
just nod, I'll fly
to Irish land
by roads and ways well
known to me.
Isolde shall be yours, sire!
I joy in this adventure!"
Curse you, you dastard!
Cursed be your head!
Vengeance! Death!
Let us both die!

BRANGAENE
(throwing herself upon Isolde
with impetuous tenderness)

O sweet one! Loved one!
Darling! Precious!
Golden lady!
Dear Isolde!
(She gradually draws Isolde toward the
couch.)
Hear me! Come now!
Sit down here!
What a dream!
What idle raving!
Why be so self-deceiving
as not to see or listen?
No matter what Sir Tristan
owes you,
how better could he pay you
than with this noblest crown of glory?
Thus does he serve
his uncle well;
he gives you the world's
most coveted prize:
all he's heir to,
truly noble,
renouncing, to place his treasure

als Königin dich zu grüßen!
(Isolde wendet sich ab.)
Und warb er Marke
dir zum Gemahl,
wie wolltest du die Wahl doch schelten,
muß er nicht wert dir gelten?
Von edler Art
und mildem Mut,
wer gliche dem Mann
an Macht und Glanz?
Dem ein hehrster Held
so treulich dient,
wer möchte sein Glück nicht teilen,
als Gattin bei ihm weilen?

ISOLDE *(starr vor sich hinblickend)*

Ungeminnt
den hehrsten Mann
stets mir nah zu sehen!
Wie könnt' ich die Qual bestehen?

BRANGÄNE

Was wähnst du, Arge?
Ungeminnt? —
(Sie nähert sich schmeichelnd und kosend Isolden.)
Wo lebte der Mann,
der dich nicht liebte?
Der Isolden säh'
und in Isolden
selig nicht ganz verging'?
Doch, der dir erkoren,
wär' er so kalt,
zög ihn von dir
ein Zauber ab:
den bösen wüßt' ich
bald zu binden.
Ihn bannte der Minne Macht.
(Mit geheimnisvoller Zutraulichkeit ganz zu Isolde.)
Kennst du der Mutter
Künste nicht?
Wähnst du, die alles
klug erwägt,
ohne Rat in fremdes Land
hätt' sie mit dir mich entsandt?

ISOLDE *(düster)*

Der Mutter Rat
gemahnt mich recht;
willkommen preis' ich
ihre Kunst: —
Rache für den Verrat —
Ruh' in der Not dem Herzen!
Den Schrein dort bring mir her!

BRANGÄNE

Er birgt, was Heil dir frommt.
(Sie holt eine kleine goldne Truhe herbei,
öffnet sie und deutet auf ihren Inhalt.)
So reihte sie die Mutter,
die mächt'gen Zaubertränke.
Für Weh und Wunden
Balsam hier;
für böse Gifte
Gegengift. *(Sie zieht ein Fläschchen hervor.)*
Den hehrsten Trank,
ich halt' ihn hier.

ISOLDE

Du irrst, ich kenn' ihn besser;
ein starkes Zeichen,
schnitt ich ihm ein.
(Sie ergreift ein Fläschchen und zeigt es.)
Der Trank ist's, der mir taugt!

BRANGÄNE *(weicht entsetzt zurück)*

Der Todestrank!
(Isolde hat sich vom Ruhebett erhoben und vernimmt mit wachsendem Schrecken den Ruf des Schiffsvolks.)

SCHIFFSVOLK *(von außen)*

Ho! He! Ha! He!
Am Untermast
die Segel ein!
Ho! He! Ha! He!

ISOLDE

Das deutet schnelle Fahrt.
Weh mir! Nahe das Land!
(Durch die Vorhänge tritt mit Ungestüm Kurwenal herein.)

VIERTER AUFTRITT

KURWENAL

Auf! Auf! Ihr Frauen!
Frisch und froh!
Rasch gerüstet!
Fertig nun, hurtig und flink!
(Gemessener.)
Und Frau Isolden
sollt' ich sagen
von Held Tristan,
meinem Herrn:
Vom Mast der Freude Flagge,
sie wehe lustig ins Land;
in Markes Königschlosse
mach' sie ihr Nahn bekannt.
Drum Frau Isolde
bät' er eilen,
fürs Land sich zu bereiten,
daß er sie könnt' geleiten.

at feet of the queen he honors.
Isolde turns away.
And if through Tristan
you wed King Mark,
why should you find fault with the choice?
Is he one not worth the prizing?
Of noble line
and gentle strength,
who equals this man
in might and fame?
Whom so great a knight
so truly serves,
who would not then share his fortune,
and dwell with such a husband?

ISOLDE *(staring vacantly)*

Unbeloved,
yet ever near
this unrivaled hero!
How could I endure the torment?

BRANGAENE

What's that, perverse one?
Unbeloved?
(She approaches Isolde coaxingly and caress-ingly.)
Where lives there a man
that would not love you?
Who that saw Isolde
would not, seeing,
dissolve in love for her?
Yet, him that is chosen,
even if cold,
drawn from your side
by magic arts,
him, though unkind,
I soon would shackle
and thrall with a mighty love.
(Coming close to Isolde with mysterious familiarity.)
Do you not know
your mother's arts?
Think you that she,
who ponders all
would have sent me void of counsel
to this strange land with you?

ISOLDE *(darkly)*

My mother's arts
I well recall;
most gladly I commend
her art.
Vengeance for who betrays,
rest for the troubled bosom!
That casket—bring it here!

BRANGAENE

It hides what does you good.
(She fetches a small gold box, opens it, and

indicates *its contents.)*
Your mother ranged them this way,
these mighty, magic potions.
For woe and wounds
the balsam here;
for deadly poison,
antidote.
(She takes out a small vial.)
The sweetest drink
I hold right here.

ISOLDE

You err, I know one better;
I marked a heavy
sign on the one.
(She seizes a vial and shows it.)
The drink here serves my turn.
(She has risen from the couch and listens with rising dread to the cries of the seamen.)

BRANGAENE *(recoils in horror)*

The drink of death!

SEAMEN *(without)*

Ho! Hey! Ha! Hey!
Stand by the mast!
Haul in the sail!
Ho! Hey! Ha! Hey!

ISOLDE

How swift our trip has been!
Woe's me! Here is the land!
Kurvenal boisterously enters through the curtains.

SCENE IV

KURVENAL

Up, up, you women!
Bright and spry!
Quickly does it!
Ready and prompt, nimble and brisk!
(Formally.)
For Dame Isolde
comes a message
my lord Tristan
would declare:
upon the mast the pennant
is gaily waving to shore;
within Mark's royal castle
your nearness now is known.
Wherefore he begs
the lady hurry,
get ready for the landing,
that then he may escort her.

ISOLDE

*(nachdem sie zuerst bet der Meldung
in Schauer zusammengefahren, gefaßt
und mit Würde)*

Herrn Tristan bringe
meinen Gruß
und meld ihm, was ich sage.
Sollt' ich zur Seit' ihm gehen,
vor König Marke zu stehen,
nicht möcht' es nach Zucht
und Fug geschehn,
empfing ich Sühne
nicht zuvor
für ungesühnte Schuld:
Drum such er meine Huld.
(Kurwenal macht eine trotzige Gebärde.)
Du merke wohl
und meld es gut!
Nicht woll' ich mich bereiten,
ans Land ihn zu begleiten;
nicht werd' ich zur Seit' ihm gehen,
vor König Marke zu stehen;
begehrte Vergessen
und Vergeben
nach Zucht und Fug
er nicht zuvor
für ungebüßte Schuld:
die böt' ihm meine Huld!

KURWENAL

Sicher wißt,
das sag' ich ihm;
nun harrt, wie er mich hört!
*(Er geht schnell zurück. Isolde eilt auf Bran-
gäne zu und umarmt sie heftig.)*

ISOLDE

Nun leb wohl, Brangäne!
Grüß mir die Welt,
grüße mir Vater und Mutter!

BRANGÄNE

Was ist? Was sinnst du?
Wolltest du fliehn?
Wohin soll ich dir folgen?

ISOLDE *(faßt sich schnell)*

Hörtest du nicht?
Hier bleib' ich,
Tristan will ich erwarten.
Getreu befolg,
was ich befehl',
den Sühnetrank
rüste schnell;
du weißt, den ich dir wies?
(Sie entnimmt dem Schrein das Fläschchen.)

BRANGÄNE

Und welchen Trank?

ISOLDE

Diesen Trank!
In die goldne Schale
gieß ihn aus;
gefüllt faßt sie ihn ganz.

BRANGÄNE

(voll Grausen das Fläschchen empfangend)

Trau' ich dem Sinn?

ISOLDE

Sei du mir treu!

BRANGÄNE

Den Trank — für wen?

ISOLDE

Wer mich betrog —

BRANGÄNE

Tristan?

ISOLDE

— trinke mir Sühne!

BRANGÄNE

(zu Isoldes Füßen stürzend)

Entsetzen! Schone mich Arme!

ISOLDE *(sehr heftig)*

Schone du mich,
untreue Magd!
Kennst du der Mutter
Künste nicht?
Wähnst du, die alles
klug erwägt,
ohne Rat in fremdes Land
hätt' sie mit dir mich entsandt?
Für Weh und Wunden
gab sie Balsam,
für böse Gifte
Gegen-Gift.
Für tiefstes Weh,
für höchstes Leid
gab sie den Todestrank.
Der Tod nun sag ihr Dank!

BRANGÄNE

(kaum ihrer mächtig)

O tiefstes Weh!

ISOLDE

Gehorchst du mir nun?

BRANGÄNE

O höchstes Leid!

ISOLDE

*(who was at first startled at the summons,
      now composedly and with dignity)*

Sir Tristan has my
greeting now:
inform him what I tell you.
If I'm to walk beside him
to stand before Mark, his monarch,
it may never be
as custom wills,
unless he finds
atonement first
for uncondoned offense:
So let him seek my grace.
(Kurvenal makes a gesture of defiance.)
Now mark me well,
report it right!
I will not now make ready
to let him hence escort me;
nor shall I parade beside him,
nor stand before Mark his monarch,
till he seek forgiveness
and forgetting
in fitting and
becoming way
for unatoned offense:
then, let him hope for grace.

KURVENAL

Rest assured,
he shall be told;
Now wait, see how he hears.
*(He retires quickly. Isolde hurries to Bran-
     gaene and embraces her warmly.)*

ISOLDE

Now farewell, Brangaene!
Greet all for me.
Greet both my father and mother.

BRANGAENE

What's this? What thoughts, these?
Would you plan flight?
To what place shall I follow?

ISOLDE *(quickly collecting herself)*

Did you not hear?
I'm staying.
Here will I wait for Tristan.
Just truly
follow my command:
prepare the peace
drink straightway.
I once showed it to you.
(She takes the vial from the casket.)

BRANGAENE

Which drink is that?

ISOLDE

Here it is!
Pour it out into
the golden cup;
it just holds it when filled.

BRANGAENE

(taking the vial in terror)

Can this be true?

ISOLDE

Mind you be true!

BRANGAENE

The drink—for whom?

ISOLDE

Him that betrayed.

BRANGAENE

Tristan?

ISOLDE

Let him atone it.

BRANGAENE

(throwing herself at Isolde's feet)

O horror! Spare me, most wretched!

ISOLDE *(very vehemently)*

Spare me instead,
disloyal girl!
Do you not know my
mother's arts?
Think you that she, who
ponders all,
would have sent me void of counsel
to this strange land with you?
For woes and wounds she
gave a balsam,
for deadly poisons
antidote.
For deepest woe,
for greatest pain
death's drink was what she gave.
Let Death now give her thanks.

BRANGAENE

(almost beside herself)

O deepest woe!

ISOLDE

Now will you obey?

BRANGAENE

O greatest pain!

ISOLDE

Bist du mir treu?

BRANGÄNE

Der Trank?

KURWENAL *(eintretend)*

Herr Tristan!
(Brangäne erhebt sich erschrocken und ver-
wirrt. Isolde sucht mit furchtbarer Anstren-
gung sich zu fassen.)

ISOLDE *(zu Kurwenal)*

Herr Tristan trete nah!

FÜNFTER AUFTRITT

Kurwenal geht wieder zurück. Brangäne,
kaum ihrer mächtig, wendet sich in den
Hintergrund. Isolde, ihr ganzes Gefühl
zur Entscheidung zusammenfassend,
schreitet langsam, mit großer Haltung,
dem Ruhebett zu, auf dessen Kopfende
sich stützend sie den Blick fest dem Ein-
gange zuwendet.

Tristan tritt ein und bleibt ehrerbietig am
Eingange stehen. Isolde is mit furcht-
barer Aufregung in seinen Anblick ver-
sunken. Langes Schweigen.

TRISTAN

Begehrt, Herrin,
was Ihr wünscht.

ISOLDE

Wüßtest du nicht,
was ich begehre,
da doch die Furcht,
mir's zu erfüllen,
fern meinem Blick dich hielt?

TRISTAN

Ehrfurcht
hielt mich in Acht.

ISOLDE

Der Ehre wenig
botest du mir;
mit offnem Hohn
verwehrtest du
Gehorsam meinem Gebot.

TRISTAN

Gehorsam einzig
hielt mich in Bann.

ISOLDE

So dankt' ich Geringes
deinem Herrn,
riet dir sein Dienst
Unsitte
gegen sein eigen Gemahl?

TRISTAN

Sitte lehrt,
wo ich gelebt:
zur Brautfahrt
der Brautwerber
meide fern die Braut.

ISOLDE

Aus welcher Sorg'?

TRISTAN

Fragt die Sitte!

ISOLDE

Da du so sittsam,
mein Herr Tristan,
auch einer Sitte
sei nun gemahnt:
den Feind dir zu sühnen,
soll er als Freund dich rühmen.

TRISTAN

Und welchen Feind?

ISOLDE

Frag deine Furcht!
Blutschuld
schwebt zwischen uns.

TRISTAN

Die ward gesühnt.

ISOLDE

Nicht zwischen uns!

TRISTAN

Im offnen Feld
vor allem Volk
ward Urfehde geschworen.

ISOLDE

Nicht da war's,
wo ich Tantris barg,
wo Tristan mir verfiel.
Da stand er herrlich,
hehr und heil;
doch was er schwur,
das schwur ich nicht:
zu schweigen hatt' ich gelernt.

ISOLDE

Will you be true?

BRANGAENE

The drink?

KURVENAL *(entering)*

Lord Tristan!

(Brangaene rises, terrified and confused. Isolde strives with a mighty effort to compose herself.)

ISOLDE *(to Kurvenal)*

Lord Tristan may approach.

SCENE V

Kurvenal retires again. Brangaene, almost beside herself, turns toward the back. Isolde, summoning all her powers to meet the crisis, walks slowly and with effort to the couch, leaning for support on its head. Her eyes are fixed on the entrance.

Tristan enters and pauses respectfully at the entrance. Isolde, a prey to violent agitation, gazes on him intently.

TRISTAN

Command, Lady,
what you wish.

ISOLDE

Do you not know
just what my wish is,
when fear you had
to undertake it
has kept you from my sight?

TRISTAN

Rev'rence
held me in awe.

ISOLDE

Scant rev'rence truly
have you shown me;
with open scorn
you have refused
obedience to my command.

TRISTAN

Obedience rather
kept me away.

ISOLDE

Small cause would I have to
thank your lord,
if serving him
makes you
discourteous toward his bride.

TRISTAN

Custom asks—
where I have lived:
ere marriage
the bride escort
keep afar from her.

ISOLDE

And on what grounds?

TRISTAN

Ask of custom!

ISOLDE

Since you're for custom,
my lord Tristan,
one other custom
you should recall:
for foe to be friendly,
let him count you as friendly.

TRISTAN

And who's the foe?

ISOLDE

Ask of your fear.
Bloodguilt
stands in the way.

TRISTAN

That was made good

ISOLDE

Not between us.

TRISTAN

In open field
before all folk
a peace compact was sworn to.

ISOLDE

But that was
not where Tantris hid
nor Tristan fell to me.
He stood there lordly,
strong and hale;
yet what he swore
I did not swear:
I'd learned that silence was best.

Da in stiller Kammer
krank er lag,
mit dem Schwerte stumm
ich vor ihm stund:
schwieg da mein Mund,
bannt' ich meine Hand —
doch was einst mit Hand
und Mund ich gelobt,
das schwur ich schweigend zu halten.
Nun will ich des Eides walten.

TRISTAN

Was schwurt Ihr, Frau?

ISOLDE

Rache für Morold!

TRISTAN

Müht Euch die?

ISOLDE

Wagst du zu höhnen?
Angelobt war er mir,
der hehre Irenheld;
seine Waffen hatt' ich geweiht;
für mich zog er zum Streit.
Da er gefallen,
fiel meine Ehr':
in des Herzens Schwere
schwur ich den Eid,
würd' ein Mann den Mord nicht sühnen,
wollt' ich Magd mich des erkühnen.
Siech und matt
in meiner Macht,
warum ich dich da nicht schlug?
Das sag dir selbst mit leichtem Fug.
Ich pflag des Wunden,
daß den Heilgesunden
rächend schlüge der Mann,
der Isolden ihm abgewann.
Dein Los nun selber
magst du dir sagen!
Da die Männer sich all ihm vertragen,
wer muß nun Tristan schlagen?

TRISTAN (bleich und düster)

War Morold dir so wert,
nun wieder nimm das Schwert
und führ es sicher und fest,
daß du nicht dir's entfallen läßt!
(Er reicht ihr sein Schwert dar.)

ISOLDE

Wie sorg' ich schlecht
um deinen Herren;
was würde König Marke sagen,
erschlüg' ich ihm
den besten Knecht,

der Kron' und Land ihm gewann,
den allertreusten Mann?
Dünkt dich so wenig,
was er dir dankt,
bringst du die Irin
ihm als Braut,
daß er nicht schölte,
schlüg' ich den Werber,
der Urfehde-Pfand
so treu ihm liefert zur Hand?
Wahre dein Schwert!
Da einst ich's schwang,
als mir die Rache
im Busen rang:
als dein messender Blick
mein Bild sich stahl,
ob ich Herrn Marke
taug' als Gemahl:
Das Schwert — da ließ ich's sinken.
Nun laß uns Sühne trinken!
(Sie winkt Brangäne. Diese schaudert zusammen, schwankt und zögert in ihrer Bewegung. Isolde treibt sie mit gesteigerter Gebärde an. Brangäne läßt sich zur Bereitung des Trankes an.)

SCHIFFSVOLK (von außen)

Ho! He! Ha! He!
Am Obermast
die Segel ein!
Ho! He! Ha! He!

TRISTAN
(aus düsterem Brüten auffahrend)

Wo sind wir?

ISOLDE

Hart am Ziel!
Tristan, gewinn' ich Sühne?
Was hast du mir zu sagen?

TRISTAN (finster)

Des Schweigens Herrin
heißt mich schweigen:
fass' ich, was sie verschweig,
verschweig' ich, was sie nicht faßt.

ISOLDE

Dein Schweigen fass' ich,
weichst du mir aus.
Weigerst du die Sühne mir?

SCHIFFSVOLK (von außen)

Ho! He! Ha! He!
(Auf Isoldes ungeduldigen Wink reicht Brangäne ihr die gefüllte Trinkschale.)

As he lay there in my
chamber sick,
mute I stood before
him with my sword:
Silent my lips,
motionless my hand—
yet what once I'd pledged
with hand and by mouth,
I swore to harbor in silence.
Now will I perform that promise.

TRISTAN

What did you swear?

ISOLDE

Vengeance for Morold!

TRISTAN

Are you concerned?

ISOLDE

Dare you to mock me?
He was fianced to me,
that gallant Irish lord;
I had consecrated his arms;
for me he went to war.
Then, with his downfall
my honor fell;
when my heart was heavy
this vow I swore:
if no man avenged his murder,
I, a maid, would dare to do so.
Sick and weak
and in my power,
why I did not slay you there,
explain yourself with easy words:
his wound I tended
so the one so healed might
pay his life to the man
who had won Isolde for bride.
Yourself may tell the
fate you're allotted.
As the men are all at peace with Tristan,
who is there left to smite him?

TRISTAN (pale and gloomy)

If Morold meant so much,
then take the sword again,
and drive it surely and straight,
that it may not escape your grasp.
(He offers her his sword.)

ISOLDE

How bad a turn
to do your master!
How do you think King Mark would take it.
if I struck down
his best of knights,

who won him both crown and land,
his truest man of all?
Think you his cause to
thank you so small,
when you have brought his
Irish bride,
he would not chide
if I slew the wooer
who faithfully brings
this peace hostage to your hand?
Put up your sword!
I grasped it once,
when thoughts of vengeance
had rent my heart,
when your measuring glance
could truly tell
whether I'd serve as
bride for King Mark:
I let the sword fall from me.
Now let us drink our friendship.
(She signs to Brangaene, who cowers and
trembles as she moves. Isolde urges her with
more impatient gestures. Brangaene sets
about preparing the drink.)

VOICES OF THE SAILORS (without)

Ho! Hey! Ha! Hey!
Stand by the mast!
Haul down the sail!
Ho! Hey! Ha! Hey!

TRISTAN
(starting from his moody silence)

Where are we?

ISOLDE

Near our goal.
Tristan, what satisfaction?
What do you have to tell me?

TRISTAN (darkly)

The queen of silence
asks for silence:
grasping what she conceals,
I hide, though, what she can't grasp.

ISOLDE

I grasp your silence
though you elude me.
Do you then refuse to pledge?

SAILORS (without)

Ho! Hey! Ha! Hey!
(On an impatient sign from Isolde, Brangaene
hands her the full goblet.)

ISOLDE
*(mit dem Becher zu Tristan tretend,
der ihr starr in die Augen blickt)*

Du hörst den Ruf?
Wir sind am Ziel.
In kurzer Frist
stehn wir *(mit leisem Hohne)*
vor König Marke.
Geleitest du mich,
dünkt dich's nicht lieb,
darfst du so ihm sagen:
„Mein Herr und Ohm,
sieh die dir an:
ein sanftres Weib
gewännst du nie.
Ihren Angelobten
erschlug ich ihr einst,
sein Haupt sandt' ich ihr heim;
die Wunde, die
seine Wehr mir schuf,
die hat sie hold geheilt.
Mein Leben lag
in ihrer Macht:
das schenkte mir
die holde Magd,
und ihres Landes
Schand' und Schmach
die gab sie mit darein,
dein Ehgemahl zu sein.
So guter Gaben
holden Dank
schuf mir ein süßer
Sühnetrank;
den bot mir ihre Huld,
zu sühnen alle Schuld."

SCHIFFSVOLK *(außen)*

Auf das Tau!
Anker los!

TRISTAN *(wild auffahrend)*

Los den Anker!
Das Steuer dem Strom!
Den Winden Segel und Mast! —
(Er entreißt ihr die Trinkschale.)
Wohl kenn' ich Irlands
Königin
und ihrer Künste
Wunderkraft.
Den Balsam nützt' ich,
den sie bot:
den Becher nehm' ich nun,
daß ganz ich heut genese.
Und achte auch
des Sühne-Eids,
den ich zum Dank dir sage!
Tristans Ehre —
höchste Treu'!

Tristans Elend —
kühnster Trotz!
Trug des Herzens!
Traum der Ahnung!
Ew'ger Trauer
einz'ger Trost:
Vergessens güt'ger Trank —
dich trink' ich sonder Wank!
(Er setzt an und trinkt.)

ISOLDE

Betrug auch hier?
Mein die Hälfte!
(Sie entwindet ihm den Becher.)
Verräter! Ich trink' sie dir!
*(Sie trinkt. Dann wirft sie die Schale fort.
Beide, von Schauer erfaßt, blicken sich mit
höchster Aufregung, doch mit starrer Haltung, unverwandt in die Augen, in deren
Ausdruck der Todestrotz bald der Liebesglut
weicht. Zittern ergreift sie. Sie fassen sich
krampfhaft an das Herz und führen die
Hand wieder an die Stirn. Dann suchen sie
sich wieder mit dem Blick, senken ihn
verwirrt und heften ihn wieder mit steigen-
der Sehnsucht aufeinander.)*
(mit bebender Stimme)

Tristan!

TRISTAN *(überströmend)*

Isolde!

ISOLDE
(an seine Brust sinkend)

Treuloser Holder!

TRISTAN
(mit Glut sie umfassend)

Seligste Frau!
*(Sie verbleiben in stummer Umarmung. Aus
der Ferne vernimmt man Trompeten.)*

RUF DER MÄNNER
(von außen auf dem Schiffe)

Heil! König Marke Heil!

BRANGÄNE

*(die, mit abgewandtem Gesicht, voll Ver-
wirrung und Schauder sich über den Bord
gelehnt hatte, wendet sich jetzt dem Anblick
des in Liebesumarmung versunkenen Paares
zu und stürzt händeringend voll Verzweif-
lung in den Vordergrund)*

Wehe! Weh!
Unabwendbar
ew'ge Not
für kurzen Tod!

ISOLDE

*(advancing with the cup to Tristan,
who gazes fixedly in her eyes)*

You hear the cries?
We have arrived:
King Mark will soon
see us *(with light scorn)*
standing before him.
And when I am there,
were it not well,
could you thus inform him:
"My lord and king,
look at her well:
a gentler wife
was never won.
Her affianced lover
I slew on a time;
I sent her home his head:
The wound that he
gave me with his sword,
she graciously made whole;
my life was fully
in her power:
the gentle maid
allowed that life,
allowed as well with
equal ease
her land's disgrace and shame,
to be your bride and queen;
in gracious thanks for
goodly gifts
mixed me a pleasant
drink of peace;
this way she showed her grace,
and wiped away my guilt."

SAILORS *(without)*

Cable up!
Anchor free!

TRISTAN *(starting wildly)*

Drop the anchor!
The helm to the stream!
The sail and mast to the wind!
(He snatches the cup from her.)
Well known to me is
Ireland's queen,
and all her cunning,
wondrous arts.
She proffered balsam,
which I used:
I'll take this beaker now
completely to recover.
Attend then to
my pledge of peace,
that thankfully I offer.
Tristan's honor—
highest faith!

Tristan's anguish—
boldest spite!
Heart's delusion!
Dream of boding!
Endless sorrow's
only rest:
Oblivion's goodly drink!
I pledge you, shrinking not!
(He puts the cup to his lips and drinks.)

ISOLDE

Betrayed here too?
Half is mine now!
(She wrests the cup from him.)
Betrayer! I drink to you!
*(She drinks, then throws away the cup. Both,
seized with shuddering, gaze with deepest
emotion, but without changing their position,
while their death-defiant expression changes
to the glow of passion. Trembling seizes
them; they convulsively clutch their hearts
and pass their hands over their brows. Their
glances again seek to meet, sink in confusion,
and once more turn with growing longing
upon each other.)*
(With trembling voice.)
Tristan!

TRISTAN *(with an outburst)*

Isolde!

ISOLDE

(sinking upon his breast)

Faithless beloved!

TRISTAN

(he embraces her passionately)

Woman most blest!
*(They remain in silent embrace.
Trumpets are heard in the distance.)*

ALL THE MEN *(without)*

Hail to King Mark, all hail!

BRANGAENE

*(Brangaene, who with averted face was lean-
ing bewildered and trembling over the side
of the ship, now turns and sees the lovers
clasped in each other's arms, and rushes
forward, wringing her hands in despair.)*

Woe is me!
Here is fatal,
endless woe
for speedy death!

Tör'ger Treue
trugvolles Werk
blüht nun jammernd empor!
(Tristan und Isolde fahren aus der Umarm-
ung auf.)

TRISTAN *(verwirrt)*

Was träumte mir
von Tristans Ehre?

ISOLDE

Was träumte mir
von Isoldes Schmach?

TRISTAN

Du mir verloren?

ISOLDE

Du mich verstoßen?

TRISTAN

Trügenden Zaubers
tückische List!

ISOLDE

Törigen Zürnens
eitles Dräun!

TRISTAN

Isolde!

ISOLDE

Tristan!

TRISTAN

Süßeste Maid!

ISOLDE

Trautester Mann!

BEIDE

Wie sich die Herzen
wogend erheben!
Wie alle Sinne
wonnig erbeben!
Sehnender Minne
schwellendes Blühen,
schmachtender Liebe
seliges Glühen!
Jach in der Brust
jauchzende Lust!
Isolde! Tristan!
Welten-entronnen,
du mir gewonnen!
Du mir einzig bewußt,
höchste Liebeslust!

(Die Vorhänge werden weit auseinandergeris-
sen; das ganze Schiff ist mit Rittern und
Schiffsvolk bedeckt, die jubelnd über Bord
winken, dem Ufer zu, das man, mit einer
hohen Felsenburg gekrönt, nahe erblickt. —
Tristan und Isolde bleiben, in ihrem gegen-
seitigen Anblick verloren, ohne Wahrneh-
mung des um sie Vorgehenden.)

BRANGÄNE
(zu den Frauen, die auf ihren Wink
aus dem Schiffsraum heraufsteigen)

Schnell, den Mantel,
den Königsschmuck!
(Zwischen Tristan und Isolde stürzend.)
Unsel'ge! Auf!
Hört, wo wir sind!
(Sie legt Isolden, die es nicht gewahrt, den
Königsmantel an.)

ALLE MÄNNER

Heil! Heil! Heil!
König Marke Heil!
Heil dem König!

KURWENAL
(lebhaft herantretend)

Heil Tristan!
Glücklicher Held!
Mit reichem Hofgesinde
dort auf Nachen
naht Herr Marke.
Hei! Wie die Fahrt ihn freut,
daß er die Braut sich freit!

TRISTAN
(in Verwirrung aufblickend)

Wer naht?

KURWENAL

Der König!

TRISTAN

Welcher König?
(Kurwenal deutet über Bord.)

ALLE MÄNNER
(die Hüte schwenkend)

Heil! König Marke Heil!
(Tristan starrt wie sinnlos nach dem Lande.)

ISOLDE *(in Verwirrung)*

Was ist, Brangäne?
Welcher Ruf?

BRANGÄNE

Isolde! Herrin!
Fassung nur heut!

Foolish, faithful
fraudulent work
blooms in wails to the skies!
(Both start from their embrace.)

TRISTAN *(confused)*

What have I dreamt
of Tristan's honor?

ISOLDE

What have I dreamt
of Isolde's shame?

TRISTAN

You—did I lose you?

ISOLDE

You—to repulse me?

TRISTAN

Fraudulent magic's
devilish guile!

ISOLDE

Idiot anger's
empty threats!

TRISTAN

Isolde!

ISOLDE

Tristan!

TRISTAN

Sweetest of maids!

ISOLDE

Truest of men!

BOTH

Ah, how our hearts are
surging and heaving;
How every sense is
joyfully throbbing!
Passionate longing,
growing and blooming;
languishing love so
blessedly glowing,
bringing my breast
jubilant joy!
Isolde! Tristan!
World, I escape you;
now I have, won you,
Tristan! Isolde!
You alone do I know!
Greatest joy of love!

The curtains are drawn wide apart; the whole ship is covered with knights and sailors who, with shouts of joy, make signs to the shore, which is now seen close at hand, crowned with a castle. Tristan and Isolde remain absorbed in mutual contemplation, perceiving nothing that is passing.

BRANGAENE

(to the women who, at a signal from her, are coming up from the cabin)

Quick, the mantle,
the royal robe!
(Rushing between Tristan and Isolde.)
Come, unblest pair!
Hear where we are!
(She puts the royal mantle on Isolde without her noticing it.)

ALL THE MEN

Hail! Hail! Hail!
Hail to King Mark, all hail!

KURVENAL *(entering briskly)*

Hail, Tristan!
Hero most blest!
He comes with rich retainers;
there aboard a barge
King Mark comes.
Hey, how well pleased he is,
coming to get his bride!

TRISTAN
(looking up confused)

Who comes?

KURVENAL

The sov'reign!

TRISTAN

Yes? What sov'reign?
(Kurvenal points over the side.)

ALL THE MEN
(waving their hats)

Hail! Hail to Mark the King!
(Tristan gazes blankly toward the shore.)

ISOLDE *(in confusion)*

What's this, Brangaene?
Why these cries?

BRANGAENE

Isolde! Mistress!
For once be calm!

ISOLDE

Wo bin ich? Leb' ich?
Ha! Welcher Trank?

BRANGÄNE (verzweiflungsvoll)

Der Liebestrank.

ISOLDE
(starrt entsetzt auf Tristan)

Tristan!

TRISTAN

Isolde!

ISOLDE

Muß ich leben?
(Sie stürzt ohnmächtig an seine Brust.)

BRANGÄNE (zu den Frauen)

Helft der Herrin!

TRISTAN

O Wonne voller Tücke!
O truggeweihtes Glücke!

ALLE MÄNNER

Kornwall Heil!
(Trompeten vom Lande her.)
(Leute sind über Bord gestiegen, andere
haben eine Brücke ausgelegt, und die Haltung aller deutet auf die soeben bevorstehende
Ankunft der Erwarteten, als der Vorhang
schnell fällt.)

ZWEITER AUFZUG

Garten mit hohen Bäumen vor dem Gemach Isoldes, zu welchem, zeitwärts ge-
legen, Stufen hinaufführen. Helle, anmu-
tige Sommernacht. An der geöffneten
Türe ist eine brennende Fackel aufge-
steckt. Jagdgetön. Brangäne, auf den Stufen am Gemach, späht dem immer ent-
fernter vernehmbaren Jagdtrosse nach.
Zu ihr tritt aus dem Gemach, feurig bewegt, Isolde.

ERSTER AUFTRITT

ISOLDE

Hörst du sie noch?
Mir schwand schon fern der Klang.

BRANGÄNE (lauschend)

Noch sind sie nah;
deutlich tönt's daher.

ISOLDE (lauschend)

Sorgende Furcht
beirrt dein Ohr.
Dich täuscht des Laubes
säuselnd Getön',
das lachend schüttelt der Wind.

BRANGÄNE

Dich täuscht des Wunsches
Ungestüm,
zu vernehmen, was du wähnst. (Sie lauscht.)
Ich höre der Hörner Schall.

ISOLDE (wieder lauschend)

Nicht Hörnerschall
tönt so hold,
des Quelles sanft
rieselnde Welle
rauscht so wonnig daher.
Wie hört' ich sie,
tosten noch Hörner?
Im Schweigen der Nacht
nur lacht mir der Quell.
Der meiner harrt
in schweigender Nacht,
als ob Hörner noch nah dir schallten,
willst du ihn fern mir halten?

BRANGÄNE

Der deiner harrt —
o hör mein Warnen! —
des harren Späher zur Nacht.
Weil du erblindet,
wähnst du den Blick
der Welt erblödet für euch?
Da dort an Schiffes Bord
von Tristans bebender Hand
die bleiche Braut,
kaum ihrer mächtig,
König Marke empfing,
als alles verwirrt
auf die Wankende sah,
der güt'ge König,
mild besorgt,
die Mühen der langen Fahrt,
die du littest, laut beklagt':
ein einz'ger war's,
ich achtet' es wohl,
der nur Tristan faßt' ins Auge.
Mit böslicher List
lauerndem Blick
sucht er in seiner Miene
zu finden, was ihm diene.
Tückisch lauschend
treff' ich ihn oft:
der heimlich euch umgarnt,
vor Melot seid gewarnt!

ISOLDE

Where am I? Living?
What was that drink?

BRANGAENE *(with despair)*

The drink of love!

ISOLDE
(stares in terror at Tristan.)

Tristan!

TRISTAN

Isolde!

ISOLDE

Must I live then?
(She sinks fainting on his breast.)

BRANGAENE *(to the women)*

Help your mistress!

TRISTAN

O rapture filled with rancor!
O bliss that's blest by treach'ry!

ALL THE MEN

Cornwall, hail!
(Trumpets are heard from the land.)
(People have climbed aboard; others have rigged a gangway; their behavior indicates their expectation of the coming arrival.)

CURTAIN

ACT II

A garden with high trees before the chamber of Isolde, which lies at one side and is approached by steps. Bright and inviting summer night. A torch burns by the open door. A hunter's horn is heard. Brangaene, standing on the steps, is watching the retreating hunt, which can still be heard. She looks back into the chamber as Isolde emerges thence in ardent animation.

SCENE I

ISOLDE

Can you still hear?
I've lost the distant sound.

BRANGAENE *(listening)*

They are still near,
plainly to be heard.

ISOLDE *(listening)*

Careful concern
deceives your ear.
You're fooled by rustling
sounds of the leaves,
that, laughing, shake in the wind.

BRANGAENE

A wild desire
deludes your mind
to interpret as you please. *(She listens.)*
I hear the resounding horns.

ISOLDE *(again listening)*

No noise of horns
sounds so sweet;
the spring, with soft
purling of waters
runs so gaily along.
If horns still blared,
how could I hear this?
In stillness of night
I hear but the spring.
The one who waits
in the silence of night,
just because of fancied horn sounds,
would you prevent approaching?

BRANGAENE

The one who waits
—oh, hear my warning—
is now awaited by spies.
Being so blinded,
do you then think
the world is purblind to you?
That day, on board the ship,
from Tristan's hands, as they shook,
King Mark received
the pale and mightless,
sad and spiritless bride;
while all were confused,
as they gazed upon you,
the gracious sov'reign,
mild and kind,
expressed to you his concern
that your journey had been long:
but one there was
—I noted it well—
who fixed eyes on Tristan only;
with evil design
cunning in gaze,
well did he search his count'nance,
to find what there might serve him.
Oft I've seen his
eavesdropping ways:
he plans some secret snare;
of Melot, then, beware!

ISOLDE

Meinst du Herrn Melot?
O, wie du dich trügst!
Ist er nicht Tristans
treuester Freund?
Muß mein Trauter mich meiden,
dann weilt er bei Melot allein.

BRANGÄNE

Was mir ihn verdächtig,
macht dir ihn teuer!
Von Tristan zu Marke
ist Melots Weg;
dort sät er üble Saat.
Die heut im Rat
dies nächtliche Jagen
so eilig schnell beschlossen,
einem edlern Wild,
als dein Wähnen meint,
gilt ihre Jägerlist.

ISOLDE

Dem Freund zulieb'
erfand diese List
aus Mitleid
Melot, der Freund.
Nun willst du den Treuen schelten?
Besser als du
sorgt er für mich;
ihm öffnet er,
was mir du sperrst.
O spare mir des Zögerns Not!
Das Zeichen, Brangäne!
O gib das Zeichen!
Lösche des Lichtes
letzten Schein!
Daß ganz sie sich neige,
winke der Nacht.
Schon goß sie ihr Schweigen
durch Hain und Haus,
schon füllt sie das Herz
mit wonnigem Graus.
O lösche das Licht nun aus,
lösche den scheuchenden Schein!
Laß meinen Liebsten ein!

BRANGÄNE

O laß die warnende Zünde,
laß die Gefahr sie dir zeigen!
O wehe! Wehe!
Ach mir Armen!
Des unseligen Trankes!
Daß ich untreu
einmal nur
der Herrin Willen trog!
Gehorcht' ich taub und blind,
dein Werk
war dann der Tod.

Doch deine Schmach,
deine schmählichste Not
mein Werk,
muß ich Schuld'ge es wissen?

ISOLDE

Dein Werk?
O tör'ge Magd!
Frau Minne kenntest du nicht?
Nicht ihres Zaubers Macht?
Des kühnsten Mutes
Königin?
Des Weltenwerdens
Walterin?
Leben und Tod
sind untertan ihr,
die sie webt aus Lust und Leid,
in Liebe wandelnd den Neid.
Des Todes Werk,
nahm ich's vermessen zur Hand,
Frau Minne hat es
meiner Macht entwandt.
Die Todgeweihte
nahm sie in Pfand,
faßte das Werk
in ihre Hand.
Wie sie es wendet,
wie sie es endet,
was sie mir küre,
wohin mich führe,
ihr ward ich zu eigen:
nun laß mich Gehorsam zeigen!

BRANGÄNE

Und mußte der Minne
tückischer Trank
des Sinnes Licht dir verlöschen,
darfst du nicht sehen,
wenn ich dich warne:
nur heute hör,
o hör mein Flehen!
Der Gefahr leuchtendes Licht,
nur heute, heut
die Fackel dort lösche nicht!

ISOLDE

Die im Busen mir
die Glut entfacht,
die mir das Herze
brennen macht,
die mir als Tag
der Seele lacht,
Frau Minne will:
es werde Nacht,
daß hell sie dorten leuchte,
(sie eilt auf die Fackel zu)
wo sie dein Licht verscheuchte.
(Sie nimmt die Fackel von der Tür.)

ISOLDE

Mean you Lord Melot?
Oh, how wrong you are!
Is he not Tristan's
truest of friends?
When my true love must shun me,
he tarries with Melot alone.

BRANGAENE

My reason for doubting
is yours for loving!
From Tristan to sov'reign
is Melot's route;
he there sows evil seed.
And those who planned
this evening hunting
with hasty-quick arrangement
look for nobler game
than your fancy deems
worthy their hunters' skill.

ISOLDE

For Tristan's sake
the plan was devised,
for Melot
pities his friend.
And will you reproach him for that?
He cares for me
better than you;
he shows to him
what you have closed.
Oh, spare delay and all its woes!
The signal, Brangaene!
Oh, give the signal!
Out with the light's last
flickering spark.
That she may enwrap us,
beckon the night!
She's poured out her silence
on grove and house;
my heart has she filled
with rapturous awe.
Oh, now let the light be quenched!
Put out its frightening glare!
Let my beloved in!

BRANGAENE

The torch of warning should stay there.
Let it illumine your danger.
O sorrow, sorrow!
Ah, poor creature!
That most unblessed of potions!
That I just once
was unfaithful
to my mistress' will!
Had I been deaf and blind,
your work
were then your death:

yet your disgrace,
your most shameful distress
I caused—
I am guilty, I own it!

ISOLDE

Your work?
O foolish maid!
Do you not know Lady Love,
nor know her magic pow'r?
The mighty queen of
valiant hearts
who rules all earthly
destiny?
Life and death
are subject to her,
these she weaves of joy and pain;
she changes hate into love.
The work of death
I boldly took into my hands,
Love's goddess, though, has
torn it from my pow'r.
The death-devoted
she took in pledge,
and seized the work
in her own hands.
Nor how she turns it,
nor how she ends it,
nor what she gives me,
nor where she leads me,
makes her less than own me:
so let me obey her orders!

BRANGAENE

And even if love's
insidious drink
puts out the light of your reason,
though you may see not,
now, when I warn you:
just hear me once,
Oh, hear my prayer!
Oh, beware: danger's awake!
Just once, this night
allow the torch, quench it not!

ISOLDE

She that fans the glow
within my breast,
she that has set my
heart on fire,
who smiles as day
upon my soul,
Love's goddess wills
it should be night,
that brightly she illumine
(She hastens toward the torch.)
the place where your light drove her.
(She takes the torch from the doorway.)

Zur Warte du:
dort wache treu!
Die Leuchte,
und wär's meines Lebens Licht —
lachend
sie zu löschen zag' ich nicht!
*(Sie wirft die Fackel zur Erde, wo sie
allmählich verlischt.)*
*(Brangäne wendet sich bestürzt ab, um auf
einer äußeren Treppe die Zinne zu ersteigen,
wo sie langsam verschwindet.)*
*(Isolde lauscht und späht, zunächst schüch-
tern, in einen Baumgang. Von wachsendem
Verlangen bewegt, schreitet sie dem Baumgang näher und späht zuversichtlicher. Sie
winkt mit einem Tuche, erst seltener, dann
häufiger, und endlich, in leidenschaftlicher
Ungeduld, immer schneller. Eine Gebärde
des plötzlichen Entzückens sagt, daß sie den
Freund in der Ferne gewahr geworden. Sie
streckt sich höher und höher, und, um besser
den Raum zu übersehen, eilt sie zur Treppe
zurück, von deren oberster Stufe aus sie dem
Herannahenden zuwinkt.)*

ZWEITER AUFTRITT

TRISTAN *(stürzt herein)*
Isolde! Geliebte!

ISOLDE
Tristan! Geliebter!
*(Stürmische Umarmungen beider, unter
denen sie in den Vordergrund gelangen.)*
Bist du mein?

TRISTAN
Hab' ich dich wieder?

ISOLDE
Darf ich dich fassen?

TRISTAN
Kann ich mir trauen?

ISOLDE
Endlich! Endlich!

TRISTAN
An meiner Brust!

ISOLDE
Fühl' ich dich wirklich?

TRISTAN
Seh' ich dich selber?

ISOLDE
Dies deine Augen?

TRISTAN
Dies dein Mund?

ISOLDE
Hier deine Hand?

TRISTAN
Hier dein Herz?

ISOLDE
Bin ich's? Bist du's?
Halt' ich dich fest?

TRISTAN
Bin ich's? Bist du's?
Ist es kein Trug?

BEIDE
Ist es kein Traum?
O Wonne der Seele,
o süße, hehrste,
kühnste, schönste,
seligste Lust!

TRISTAN
Ohne Gleiche!

ISOLDE
Überreiche!

TRISTAN
Überselig!

ISOLDE
Ewig!

TRISTAN
Ewig!

ISOLDE
Ungeahnte,
nie gekannte!

TRISTAN
Überschwenglich
hoch erhabne!

ISOLDE
Freudejauchzen!

TRISTAN
Lustentzücken!

So go on guard:
and keep true watch!
The splendor
—though it were my light of life—
laughing,
without tremor I would quench!
(*She throws the torch to the ground, where it
gradually goes out. Brangaene turns dis-
tressedly away in order to get upon the
parapet by an outer staircase, where she
slowly disappears. Isolde listens and looks,
at first timidly, down the avenue of trees.
Stirred by increasing longing, she goes nearer
to the avenue and looks out more boldly.
She waves her kerchief, at first from time
to time, then oftener, finally with passionate
impatience, faster and faster. A gesture of
sudden delight shows that she has perceived
her lover in the distance. She raises herself
higher and higher, the better to overlook the
place, then hurries back to the steps, from
the top of which she beckons to him as he
approaches.*)

SCENE II

TRISTAN (*rushing in*)

Isolde! Beloved!

ISOLDE

Tristan! Beloved!
(*They embrace passionately, then come down
to the front.*)
Are you mine?

TRISTAN

Now do I have you?

ISOLDE

Dare I embrace you?

TRISTAN

Can I believe it?

ISOLDE

No more waiting!

TRISTAN

Come to my breast!

ISOLDE

Now do I touch you?

TRISTAN

Whom do I see here?

ISOLDE

Are these your eyes?

TRISTAN

This your mouth?

ISOLDE

Is this your hand?

TRISTAN

Here your heart?

ISOLDE

Is it I? Is't you
here in my arms?

TRISTAN

Is it I? Is't you?
Is it no trick?

BOTH

Is it no dream?
Glorious rapture!
O sweetest, highest,
keenest, fairest,
blessedest joy!

TRISTAN

Without equal!

ISOLDE

Beyond riches!

TRISTAN

More than blessed!

ISOLDE

Endless!

TRISTAN

Endless!

ISOLDE

Never dreamed of!
Never known of!

TRISTAN

Exaltation
never equaled!

ISOLDE

Joy-exulting!

TRISTAN

Raptured pleasure!

BEIDE

Himmelhöchstes
Weltentrücken!
Mein! { Tristan / Isolde } mein!
Mein und dein!
Ewig, ewig ein!

ISOLDE

Wie lange fern!
Wie fern so lang!

TRISTAN

Wie weit so nah!
So nah wie weit!

ISOLDE

O Freundesfeindin,
böse Ferne!
Träger Zeiten
zögernde Länge!

TRISTAN

O Weit' und Nähe,
hart entzweite!
Holde Nähe!
Öde Weite!

ISOLDE

Im Dunkel du,
im Lichte ich!

TRISTAN

Das Licht! Das Licht!
O dieses Licht,
wie lang verlosch es nicht!
Die Sonne sank,
der Tag verging,
doch seinen Neid
erstickt' er nicht:
sein scheuchend Zeichen
zündet er an
und steckt's an der Liebsten Türe,
daß nicht ich zu ihr führe.

ISOLDE

Doch der Liebsten Hand
löschte das Licht;
wes die Magd sich wehrte,
scheut' ich mich nicht:
in Frau Minnes Macht und Schutz
bot ich dem Tage Trutz!

TRISTAN

Dem Tage! Dem Tage!
Dem tückischen Tage,
dem härtesten Feinde
Haß und Klage!

Wie du das Licht,
o könnt' ich die Leuchte,
der Liebe Leiden zu rächen,
dem frechen Tage verlöschen!
Gibt's eine Not,
gibt's eine Pein,
die er nicht weckt
mit seinem Schein?
Selbst in der Nacht
dämmernder Pracht
hegt ihn Liebchen am Haus,
streckt mir drohend ihn aus!

ISOLDE

Hegt ihn die Liebste
am eignen Haus,
im eignen Herzen
hell und kraus
hegt' ihn trotzig
einst mein Trauter:
Tristan — der mich betrog!
War's nicht der Tag,
der aus ihm log,
als er nach Irland
werbend zog,
für Marke mich zu frein,
dem Tod die Treue zu weihn?

TRISTAN

Der Tag! Der Tag,
der dich umgliß,
dahin, wo sie
der Sonne glich,
in höchster Ehren
Glanz und Licht
Isolde mir entrückt'!
Was mir das Auge
so entzückt',
mein Herze tief
zur Erde drückt':
in lichten Tages Schein
wie war Isolde mein?

ISOLDE

War sie nicht dein,
die dich erkor?
Was log der böse
Tag dir vor,
daß, die für dich beschieden,
die Traute du verrietest?

TRISTAN

Was dich umgliß
mit hehrster Pracht,
der Ehre Glanz,
des Ruhmes Macht,
an sie mein Herz zu hangen,
hielt mich der Wahn gefangen.

BOTH

Heaven-high
above all earthly!
Mine! {Tristan! / Isolde!} Mine!
Mine and yours!
Ever, ever one!

ISOLDE

How long afar!
How far so long!

TRISTAN

So far, yet near!
So near, yet far!

ISOLDE

O foe to friendship,
wicked distance!
Slothful hours of
tedious slowness!

TRISTAN

But far, or near you,
hard division!
Precious nearness!
Barren distance!

ISOLDE

The dark for you,
the light for me!

TRISTAN

The light! The light!
O troubling light,
how long before it's out?
The sun has sunk,
the day has fled,
yet out of spite
the light remains:
it lights a fearful
sign which it set
beside my beloved's doorway,
so that I may not reach her.

ISOLDE

Yet the loved one's hand
smothered the light;
what my handmaid turned from,
I did not fear.
Through love's guarding care and might
I here defy the day!

TRISTAN

The daylight! The daylight!
To treacherous daylight,
my bitterest foe,
laments and loathing!

As you the light,
Oh, could I extinguish
the lording day with its beacons,
thus venging love for its suff'rings!
Is there one woe,
is there one pain
that is not wakened
by its glare?
Even in night's
splendor of dusk,
first she took in this bane,
then she proffered it me.

ISOLDE

What if I took in
the baneful light,
defiantly my
loved one harbored
this light within
his bosom—
Tristan, who tricked his love!
Was't not the day
that lied through him
when he sought Ireland
for his king,
and I was wooed for Mark
that thus the true one might die?

TRISTAN

The day! The day
has made you glow
and shine splendid
in honor's light,
but infinitely
far removed,
just like the sun itself!
The sight that so
entranced my eye,
weighed down my heart
to earthy depths:
in brilliant light of day,
how could Isold' be mine?

ISOLDE

Was she not yours
who called you hers?
What lies did wicked
day devise
that made you trick the true one
who chose you as her loved one?

TRISTAN

A splendid aura
gave you grace:
your honor's light,
your high renown,
to make my heart a captive—
these seized my ardent fancy.

Die mit des Schimmers
hellstem Schein
mir Haupt und Scheitel
licht beschien,
der Welten-Ehren
Tagessonne,
mit ihrer Strahlen
eitler Wonne,
durch Haupt und Scheitel
drang mir ein
bis in des Herzens
tiefsten Schrein.
Was dort in keuscher Nacht
dunkel verschlossen wacht',
was ohne Wiss' und Wahn
ich dämmernd dort empfahn:
ein Bild, das meine Augen
zu sehn sich nicht getrauten,
von des Tages Schein betroffen
lag mir's da schimmernd offen.
Was mir so rühmlich
schien und hehr,
das rühmt' ich hell
vor allem Heer;
vor allem Volke
pries ich laut
der Erde schönste
Königsbraut.
Dem Neid, den mir
der Tag erweckt';
dem Eifer, den
mein Glücke schreckt';
der Mißgunst, die mir Ehren
und Ruhm begann zu schweren:
denen bot ich Trotz,
und treu beschloß,
um Ehr' und Ruhm zu wahren,
nach Irland ich zu fahren.

ISOLDE

O eitler Tagesknecht!
Getäuscht von ihm,
der dich getäuscht,
wie mußt' ich liebend
um dich leiden,
den, in des Tages
falschem Prangen,
von seines Gleißens
Trug befangen,
dort, wo ihn Liebe
heiß umfaßte,
im tiefsten Herzen
hell ich haßte.
Ach, in des Herzens Grunde
wie schmerzte tief die Wunde!
Den dort ich heimlich barg,
wie dünkt' er mich so arg,
wenn in des Tages Scheine
die treu gehegte Eine

der Liebe Blicken schwand,
als Feind nur vor mir stand!
Das als Verräter
dich mir wies,
dem Licht des Tages
wollt' ich entfliehn,
dorthin in die Nacht
dich mit mir ziehn,
wo der Täuschung Ende
mein Herz mir verhieß;
wo des Trugs geahnter
Wahn zerrinne;
dort dir zu trinken
ew'ge Minne,
mit mir dich in Verein
wollt' ich dem Tode weihn.

TRISTAN

In deiner Hand
den süßen Tod,
als ich ihn erkannt,
den sie mir bot;
als mir die Ahnung
hehr und gewiß
zeigte, was mir
die Sühne verhieß:
da erdämmerte mild
erhabner Macht
im Busen mir die Nacht;
mein Tag war da vollbracht.

ISOLDE

Doch ach, dich täuschte
der falsche Trank,
daß dir von neuem
die Nacht versank;
dem einzig am Tode lag,
den gab er wieder dem Tag!

TRISTAN

O Heil dem Tranke!
Heil seinem Saft!
Heil seines Zaubers
hehrer Kraft!
Durch des Todes Tor,
wo er mir floß,
weit und offen
er mir erschloß,
darin ich sonst nur träumend gewacht,
das Wunderreich der Nacht.
Von dem Bild in des Herzens
bergendem Schrein
scheucht' er des Tages
täuschenden Schein,
daß nachtsichtig mein Auge
wahr es zu sehen tauge.

These with their brilliant
rays of light
shone lightly on my
head and crown;
but day's bright sun of
worldly honor
with its resplendent,
empty rapture
pierced strongly through my
crown and head
down to my heart's most
hidden shrine.
The chaste night held it there,
where, locked in dark, it woke,
this thing I had not dreamed,
just dimly had perceived,
a picture that my eyes did not
dare so much as gaze on,
when a ray of day revealed it,
and made it shine before me.
What seemed so
glorious-sublime
I lauded forth to
all the host;
to all the folk I
cried your praise
as bride on earth most
fit for kings.
The spite—the envy
waked by day;
the passion that
my luck dismayed—
the ill-will that began to
oppress my fame and honor:
I defied them all,
and undertook
to save that fame and honor
by faring back to Ireland.

ISOLDE

O idle slave of day!
Deceived by it,
deceived, like you,
how I have loved you
and so suffered,
whom, in the day's
deceitful splendor,
enthralled and
caught in glitt'ring fetters,
there, where a fiery
love embraced you,
within my hottest
heart I hated!
Ah, in my bosom's center,
how deep the wound was smarting!
the one there concealed,
how wicked did he seem
when in the day's effulgence
the one so truly cherished

had lost his loving look,
the foe, only, remained!
That which had showed you
false to me,
the light of day,
I now wished to flee,
and deep into night
draw you with me,
where my heart foretold me
the error would end;
where all feared deceit and
fraud would vanish,
there would I drink to you
love eternal.
I wished, joined into one,
we might be pledged in death.

TRISTAN

The time when I
did recognize
the sweet death you proffered
in the cup,
when intuition
surely and well
showed what the peace
pledge promised my hope:
then there came as a dawn
within my bosom,
mild, exalted night.
My day was then fulfilled.

ISOLDE

But ah, that false drink
deceived you too,
so that your night
vanished once again:
and one at the door of death
was brought again to the day!

TRISTAN

All hail the potion!
Hail to its juice!
Hail to its lofty
magical might!
Through the door of death,
where I quaffed it,
wide it opened
its wondrous realm,
wherein I'd wandered only in dreams,
the wonderland of night.
From the picture within my
heart's secret shrine,
gone was the lying
glitter of day:
my eyes, used to the darkness
now could perceive it truly.

ISOLDE

Doch es rächte sich
der verscheuchte Tag;
mit deinen Sünden
Rat's er pflag:
was dir gezeigt
die dämmernde Nacht,
an des Tag-Gestirnes
Königsmacht
mußtest du's übergeben,
um einsam
in öder Pracht
schimmernd dort zu leben.
Wie ertrug ich's nur?
Wie ertrag' ich's noch?

TRISTAN

O, nun waren wir
Nacht-Geweihte!
Der tückische Tag,
der Neid-bereite,
trennen konnt' uns sein Trug,
doch nicht mehr täuschen sein Lug!
Seine eitle Pracht,
seinen prahlenden Schein
verlacht, wem die Nacht
den Blick geweiht:
seines flackernden Lichtes
flüchtige Blitze
blenden uns nicht mehr.
Wer des Todes Nacht
liebend erschaut,
wem sie ihr tief'
Geheimnis vertraut:
des Tages Lügen,
Ruhm und Ehr',
Macht und Gewinn,
so schimmernd hehr,
wie eitler Staub der Sonnen
sind sie vor dem zersponnen!
In des Tages eitlem Wähnen
bleibt ihm ein einzig Sehnen —
das Sehnen hin
zur heil'gen Nacht,
wo ur-ewig,
einzig wahr
Liebeswonne ihm lacht!
(*Tristan zieht Isolde sanft zur Seite auf eine Blumenbank nieder, senkt sich vor ihr auf die Knie und schmiegt sein Haupt in ihren Arm.*)

BEIDE

O sink hernieder,
Nacht der Liebe,
gib Vergessen,
daß ich lebe;

nimm mich auf
in deinen Schoß,
löse von
der Welt mich los!

TRISTAN

Verloschen nun
die letzte Leuchte;

ISOLDE

was wir dachten,
was uns deuchte;

TRISTAN

all Gedenken —

ISOLDE

all Gemahnen —

BEIDE

heil'ger Dämm'rung
hehres Ahnen
löscht des Wähnens Graus
welterlösend aus.

ISOLDE

Barg im busen
uns sich die Sonne,
leuchten lachend
Sterne der Wonne.

TRISTAN

Von deinem Zauber
sanft umsponnen,
vor deinen Augen
süß zerronnen;

ISOLDE

Herz an Herz dir,
Mund an Mund;

TRISTAN

eines Atems
ein'ger Bund;

BEIDE

bricht mein Blick sich
wonnerblindet.
erbleicht die Welt
mit ihrem Blenden:

ISOLDE

die uns der Tag
trügend erhellt,

TRISTAN

zu täuschendem Wahn
entgegengestellt,

ISOLDE

But affrighted day
took its due revenge;
and with your sins it
joined in league:
what you were shown
in shadowing night,
to the kingly might of
day's bright star,
you were forced to surrender,
and there now
it lives in lone,
lovely, barren splendor.
How have I borne this?
Can I bear it still?

TRISTAN

Oh, now we are night
consecrated!
Malevolent day,
disposed to envy,
though it part us through fraud
can trick us no more by lies!
All its idle pomp,
its braggardly show
is scorned by the man
with eyes night-blessed:
and the fugitive flashes
cast by its lightning
blind our eyes no more.
He who finds death's night
dear to his view,
he who has plumbed
the secrets and depths,
will hold day's falsehood,
fame and name,
honor and gain
—though dazzling bright—
as idle motes in sunlight,
which drift away and vanish.
Mid the daylight's idle fancies
he has one only longing,
a longing for
the holy night,
where forever,
solely true,
love and rapture await!
(Tristan draws Isolde gently down on a
flowery bank at one side, sinks on his knees
before her and rests his head on her arm.)

BOTH

Oh, close around us,
night of rapture,
grant forgetting,
that I'm living,

take me up,
unto your breast;
set me free
now from the world!

TRISTAN

Extinguished is
the light's last lantern.

ISOLDE

All our thinking,
all appearance.

TRISTAN

All remembrance.

ISOLDE

All recalling.

BOTH

Holy twilight's
lofty visions
make vain terrors melt,
setting spirit free.

ISOLDE

When the sun lies
hid in our bosoms,
laughing stars shine
forth in their rapture.

TRISTAN

Your gentle magic
flows about us,
before your eyes
so sweetly swooning.

ISOLDE

Heart on heart and
mouth on mouth.

TRISTAN

Merged in one, in
one sole breath.

BOTH

Eyes are dazed by
blinding rapture,
earth pales away
with all its glitter.

ISOLDE

Giv'n by the day
just to mislead.

TRISTAN

All earthly illusion
here I defy:

BEIDE

selbst dann
bin ich die Welt:
Wonne-hehrstes Weben,
Leibe-heiligstes Leben,
Nie-wieder-Erwachens
wahnlos
hold bewußter Wunsch.
*(Tristan und Isolde versinken wie in gänz-
liche Entrücktheit, in der sie, Haupt an
Haupt auf die Blumenbank zurückgelehnt,
verweilen.)*

BRANGÄNES STIMME
(von der Zinne her)

Einsam wachend
in der Nacht,
wem der Traum
der Liebe lacht,
hab' der Einen
Ruf in acht,
die den Schläfern
Schlimmes ahnt,
bange zum
Erwachen mahnt.
Habet acht!
Habet acht!
Bald entweicht die Nacht.

ISOLDE

Lausch, Geliebter!

TRISTAN

Laß mich sterben!

ISOLDE
(allmählich sich ein wenig erhebend)

Neid'sche Wache!

TRISTAN

Nie erwachen!

ISOLDE

Doch der Tag
muß Tristan wecken?

TRISTAN
(ein wenig das Haupt erhebend)

Laß den Tag
dem Tode weichen!

ISOLDE

Tag und Tod
mit gleichen Streichen
sollten unsre
Lieb' erreichen?

TRISTAN
(sich mehr aufrichtend)

Unsre Liebe?
Tristans Liebe?
Dein' und mein',
Isoldes Liebe?
Welches Todes Streichen
könnte je sie weichen?
Stünd' er vor mir,
der mächt'ge Tod,
wie er mir Leib
und Leben bedroht',
die ich so willig
die Liebe lasse,
wie wäre seinen Streichen
die Liebe selbst zu erreichen?
Stürb' ich nun ihr,
der so gern ich sterbe,
wie könnte die Liebe
mit mir sterben,
die ewig lebende
mit mir enden?
Doch stürbe nie seine Liebe,
wie stürbe dann Tristan
seiner Liebe?

ISOLDE

Doch unsre Liebe,
heißt sie nicht Tristan
und — Isolde?
Dies süße Wörtlein: und,
was es bindet,
der Liebe Bund,
wenn Tristan stürb',
zerstört' es nicht der Tod?

TRISTAN

Was stürbe dem Tod,
als was uns stört,
was Tristan wehrt,
Isolde immer zu lieben,
ewig ihr nur zu leben?

ISOLDE

Doch dieses Wörtlein: und —
wär' es zerstört,
wie anders als
mit Isoldes eignem Leben
wär' Tristan der Tod gegeben?
*(Tristan zieht, mit bedeutungsvoller Gebärde,
Isolde sanft an sich.)*

TRISTAN

So stürben wir,
um ungetrennt,
ewig einig
ohne End',
ohn' Erwachen,

BOTH

I myself
am the world.
Joy that weaves our rapture,
Life of love at its holiest,
no more reawak'ning,
dreamless,
sweet, awaited wish.
*(Completely carried away, Tristan and Isolde
sink down and remain lying on the flowery
bank, their heads side by side.)*

BRANGAENE
(from the turret, invisible)

While I watch
alone by night:
you who bask
in dreams of love,
give my only
cry your heed,
for it warns of
woe to come.
Oh, beware,
I urge you wake!
Have a care!
Soon the night will fade!

ISOLDE

Hark, beloved!

TRISTAN

Let me die now!

ISOLDE
(gently raising herself a little)

Envious watcher!

TRISTAN

No more waking!

ISOLDE

Must the day
not waken Tristan?

TRISTAN
(raising his head a little)

Let the day
to death be given!

ISOLDE

Would not day
and death as equals
overtake our
love and rend it?

TRISTAN
(raising himself slightly)

Love as ours is?
Tristan's passion?
Yours and mine,
Isolde's passion?
Even though Death lashed it,
could it ever weaken?
Were mighty Death
to stand here now,
threatening both
my life and my limbs,
trying to will me
to love no longer,
how could he ever hope to
destroy the love that I harbor?
Dying for that I'd so gladly die for,
how could such a love then
die when I do,
how could the endlessly
living perish?
Yet if his love could not perish,
could Tristan die yoked to
love eternal?

ISOLDE

Yet, may we name it,
this love, as Tristan
and Isolde?
This little, sweet word "and":
how it binds us
—this bond of love—
if Tristan died
would death not murder this?

TRISTAN

What could death destroy
but what prevents
your Tristan's heart
from ever loving his Isold',
ever living for Isold'?

ISOLDE

Yet, how to cancel this
little word "and":
how otherwise than
with Isold's very life were
death to be given Tristan?
*(Tristan, with expressive gestures, draws
Isolde gently to him.)*

TRISTAN

But should we die,
we would not part,
joined forever,
without end,
never waking,

ohn' Erbangen,
namenlos
in Lieb' umfangen,
ganz uns selbst gegeben,
der Liebe nur zu leben!

ISOLDE
*(wie in sinnender Entrücktheit
zu ihm aufblickend)*

So stürben wir,
um ungetrennt —

TRISTAN

ewig einig
ohne End' —

ISOLDE

ohn' Erwachen —

TRISTAN

ohn' Erbangen —

BEIDE

namenlos
in Lieb' umfangen
ganz uns selbst gegeben,
der Liebe nur zu leben!
*(Isolde neigt wie überwältigt das Haupt an
seine Brust.)*

BRANGÄNES STIMME *(wie vorher)*

Habet acht!
Habet acht!
Schon weicht dem Tag die Nacht.

TRISTAN
(lächelnd zu Isolde geneigt)

Soll ich lauschen?

ISOLDE
(schwärmerisch zu Tristan aufblickend)

Laß mich sterben!

TRISTAN *(ernster)*

Muß ich wachen?

ISOLDE *(bewegter)*

Nie erwachen!

TRISTAN

Soll der Tag
noch Tristan wecken?

ISOLDE

Laß den Tag
dem Tode weichen!

TRISTAN

Des Tages Dräuen
nun trotzten wir so?

ISOLDE
(mit wachsender Begeisterung)

Seinem Trug ewig zu fliehn.

TRISTAN

Sein dämmernder Schein
verscheuchte uns nie?

ISOLDE
(mit großer Gebärde ganz sich erhebend)

Ewig währ' uns die Nacht!
*(Tristan folgt ihr, sie umfangen sich in
schwärmerischer Begeisterung.)*

BEIDE

O ew'ge Nacht,
süße Nacht!
Hehr erhabne
Liebesnacht!
Wen du umfangen,
wem du gelacht,
wie wär' ohne Bangen
aus dir er je erwacht?
Nun banne das Bangen,
holder Tod,
sehnend verlangter
Liebestod!
In deinen Armen,
dir geweiht,
ur-heilig Erwarmen,
von Erwachens Not befreit!

TRISTAN

Wie sie fassen,
wie sie lassen,
diese Wonne —

BEIDE

Fern der Sonne,
fern der Tage
Trennungsklage!

ISOLDE

Ohne Wähnen —

TRISTAN

sanftes Sehnen;

ISOLDE

ohne Bangen —

TRISTAN

süß Verlangen.
Ohne Wehen —

never fearing,
nameless there,
in love enfolded,
each to each belonging,
with love alone our life source!

ISOLDE
*(looking up at him
in thoughtful absorption)*

But should we die,
we would not part . . .

TRISTAN

joined forever,
without end . . .

ISOLDE

never waking . . .

TRISTAN

never fearing . . .

BOTH

nameless there,
in love enfolded,
each to each belonging,
with love alone our life source!
*(Isolde, as if overpowered, droops her head
upon his breast.)*

BRANGAENE'S VOICE *(as before)*

Have a care!
Have a care!
The night gives place to day!

TRISTAN
(bends smilingly down to Isolde)

Shall I listen?

ISOLDE
(gazing fondly at Tristan)

Let me die thus!

TRISTAN *(more gravely)*

Must I waken?

ISOLDE *(more affected)*

Never waken!

TRISTAN

Must the day
yet waken Tristan?

BOTH

Let the day
to death surrender!

TRISTAN

But shall we now give
defiance to day?

ISOLDE
(with rising ecstasy)

Could we fly far from its fraud!

TRISTAN

The light of its dawn would never bring fear.

ISOLDE
(rising to her feet)

Let the night never end!
*(Tristan follows her; they embrace in a fond
ecstasy.)*

BOTH

O endless night,
blissful night!
noble-lofty
night of love!
Those whom you compass,
those whom you love,
could they without dismay
waken from your sleep?
Let fear now be banished,
gracious death,
yearningly longed-for
love-in-death.
Within your arms
we are yours,
warmth, prime and most holy,
from awakening's woes set free!

TRISTAN

How to grasp it,
how to lose it.
This enchantment . . .

BOTH

Far from sunlight,
far from daylight's
parting outcries!

ISOLDE

No illusions, . . .

TRISTAN

. . . tender yearnings!

ISOLDE

All fear ended, . . .

TRISTAN

. . . sweet desiring!
No more sorrow, . . .

BEIDE
hehr Vergehen.

ISOLDE
Ohne Schmachten —

BEIDE
hold Umnachten.

TRISTAN
Ohne Meiden —

BEIDE
ohne Scheiden,
traut allein,
ewig heim,
in ungemeßnen Räumen
übersel'ges Träumen.

ISOLDE
Du Isolde,

TRISTAN
Tristan du,

ISOLDE
Tristan ich,

TRISTAN
ich Isolde,

ISOLDE
nicht mehr Isolde!

TRISTAN
nicht mehr Tristan!

BEIDE
Ohne Nennen,
ohne Trennen,
neu' Erkennen,
neu' Entbrennen;
ewig endlos,
ein-bewußt:
heiß erglühter Brust
höchste Liebeslust!
(Sie bleiben in verzückter Stellung.)
(Brangäne stößt einen grellen Schrei aus.)
(Kurwenal stürzt mit entblößtem Schwerte
herein.)

DRITTER AUFTRITT

KURWENAL
Rette dich, Tristan!
(Er blickt mit Entsetzen hinter sich in die

Szene zurück. Marke, Melot und Hofleute,
in Jägertracht, kommen aus dem Baumgange
lebhaft nach dem Vordergrunde und halten
entsetzt der Gruppe der Liebenden gegen-
über an. Brangäne kommt zuleich von der
Zinne herab und stürzt auf Isolde zu. Diese,
von unwillkürlicher Scham ergriffen, lehnt
sich, mit abgewandtem Gesicht, auf die
Blumenbank. Tristan, in ebenfalls unwillkürlicher Bewegung, streckt mit dem einen
Arm den Mantel breit aus, so daß er Isolde
vor den Blicken der Ankommenden verdeckt.
In dieser Stellung verbleibt er längere Zeit,
unbeweglich den starren Blick auf die Männer gerichtet, die in verschiedener Bewegung
die Augen auf ihn heften. Morgendämmer-
ung.)

TRISTAN
Der öde Tag
zum letztenmal!

MELOT (zu Marke)
Das sollst du, Herr, mir sagen,
ob ich ihn recht verklagt?
Das dir zum Pfand ich gab,
ob ich mein Haupt gewahrt?
Ich zeigt' ihn dir
in offner Tat:
Namen und Ehr'
hab' ich getreu
vor Schande dir bewahrt.

MARKE
(nach tiefer Erschütterung,
mit bebender Stimme)
Tatest du's wirklich?
Wähnst du das?
Sieh ihn dort,
den treusten aller Treuen;
blick' auf ihn,
den freundlichsten der Freunde:
seiner Treue
freiste Tat
traf mein Herz
mit feindlichstem Verrat!
Trog mich Tristan,
sollt' ich hoffen,
was sein Trügen
mir getroffen,
sei durch Melots Rat
redlich mir bewahrt?

TRISTAN
Tagsgespenster!
Morgenträume!
Täuschend und wüst!
Entschwebt! Entweicht!

BOTH

Noble surcease!

ISOLDE

No more pining . . .

BOTH

. . . night-encompassed.

TRISTAN

No more parting . . .

BOTH

. . . no more sundered,
yet alone,
always home,
in realms of endless grandeur,
dream of blessed wonder!

ISOLDE

You Isolde . . .

TRISTAN

. . . you Tristan!

ISOLDE

Tristan I, . . .

TRISTAN

. . . I Isolde!

ISOLDE

No more Isolde!

TRISTAN

No more Tristan!

BOTH

No more naming,
no more parting,
newborn knowledge,
newborn ardors,
ever endless,
both one mind:
hotly glowing breast,
love's supreme delight!
(They keep their positions, as if entranced.
Brangaene utters a piercing shriek, as Kurvenal enters with drawn sword.)

SCENE III

KURVENAL

Save yourself, Tristan!
(He looks off stage behind him in great alarm.

Mark, Melot, and courtiers, in hunting dress,
come quickly from the avenue toward the
front, and pause in amazement before the
lovers. In the meantime Brangaene descends
from the turret and rushes toward Isolde,
who, with instinctive shame, leans with
averted face upon the flowery bank. Tristan,
with an equally instinctive movement, with
one arm spreads his cloak so as to conceal
Isolde from the eyes of the newcomers. In
this position he remains for some time, his
eyes steadily fixed upon the men who look
at him with varied emotions. Morning dawns.)

TRISTAN

This dreary day,
last time of all!

MELOT (to Mark)

Now will you, Lord, please tell me
if I accused aright?
and what I staked as pledge,
my head, is it still mine?
I've shown him in
the very act.
Well did I watch,
saving your honored
name and fame from shame.

MARK
(violently affected,
then with trembling voice)

Have you though, really?
Is it true?
See him there,
the truest of all true ones;
look on him,
the best of friends in friendship:
yet his best, his
freest deed
was to stab
my heart by playing false!
If he tricked me,
shall I hope then
what his treachery had ruined
might through Melot be
somehow truly saved?

TRISTAN

Daytime phantoms!
Morning dream-stuff!
Lying and vain!
Disperse! Dissolve!

MARKE (*mit tiefer Ergriffenheit*)

Mir dies?
Dies, Tristan, mir? —
Wohin nun Treue,
da Tristan mich betrog?
Wohin nun Ehr'
und echte Art,
da aller Ehren Hort,
da Tristan sie verlor?
Die Tristan sich
zum Schild erkor,
wohin ist Tugend
nun entflohn,
da meinen Freund sie flieht,
da Tristan mich verriet?
(*Tristan senkt langsam den Blick zu Boden;
in seinen Mienen ist, während Marke fort-
fährt, zunehmende Trauer zu lesen.*)
Wozu die Dienste
ohne Zahl,
der Ehren Ruhm,
der Größe, Macht,
die Marken du gewannst;
mußt' Ehr' und Ruhm,
Größ' und Macht,
mußte die Dienste
ohne Zahl
dir Markes Schmach bezahlen?
Dünkte zu wenig
dich sein Dank,
daß, was du ihm erworben,
Ruhm und Reich,
er zu Erb' und Eigen dir gab?
Da kinderlos einst
schwand sein Weib,
so liebt' er dich,
daß nie aufs neu'
sich Marke wollt' vermählen.
Da alles Volk
zu Hof und Land
mit Bitt' und Dräuen
in ihn drang,
die Königin dem Lande,
die Gattin sich zu kiesen;
da selber du
den Ohm beschworst,
des Hofes Wunsch,
des Landes Willen
gütlich zu erfüllen;
in Wehr wider Hof und Land,
in Wehr selbst gegen dich,
mit List und Güte
weigerte er sich,
bis, Tristan, du ihm drohtest,
für immer zu meiden
Hof und Land,
würdest du selber
nicht entsandt,

dem König die Braut zu frein.
Da ließ er's denn so sein. —
Dies wundervolle Weib,
das mir dein Mut gewann,
wer durft' es sehen,
wer es kennen,
wer mit Stolze
sein es nennen,
ohne selig sich zu preisen?
Der mein Wille
nie zu nahen wagte,
der mein Wunsch
ehrfurchtscheu entsagte,
die so herrlich
hold erhaben
mir die Seele
mußte laben,
trotz Feind und Gefahr,
die fürstliche Braut
brachtest du mir dar.
Nun, da durch solchen
Besitz mein Herz
du fühlsamer schufst
als sonst dem Schmerz,
dort, wo am weichsten,
zart und offen,
würd' ich getroffen,
nie zu hoffen,
daß je ich könnte gesunden:
warum so sehrend,
Unseliger,
dort nun mich verwunden?
Dort mit der Waffe
quälendem Gift,
das Sinn und Hirn
mir sengend versehrt,
das mir dem Freund
die Treue verwehrt,
mein offnes Herz
erfüllt mit Verdacht,
daß ich nun heimlich
in dunkler Nacht
den Freund lauschend beschleiche,
meiner Ehren Ende erreiche?
Die kein Himmel erlöst,
warum mir diese Hölle?
Die kein Elend sühnt,
warum mir diese Schmach?
Den unerforschlich tief
geheimnisvollen Grund,
wer macht der Welt ihn kund?

TRISTAN
(*mitleidig das Auge zu Marke erhebend*)

O König, das
kann ich dir nicht sagen;
und was du frägst,
das kannst du nie erfahren.

MARK (*in sorrowful reproach*)

You, though!
This, Tristan, to me?
Where then is truth found,
if Tristan has betrayed?
Where are good faith
and honor gone,
when he who was their guard,
my Tristan, lost them all?
And what he chose
himself for shield,
his virtue, now, where
has it flown,
since it has fled my friend,
my Tristan, who betrayed?
*Tristan slowly drops his eyes to the ground;
his face expresses his increasing sorrow as
Mark continues.*
Whereto your services
untold,
that honor, fame,
and puissant might
you won for Mark, your king;
if honor, fame,
puissant might,
if all your services untold
be paid with Mark's dishonor?
Thought you so little
of his thanks,
that when you gained and gave him
fame and kingdom
he made you heir to it all?
When childless he lost
once his wife,
he loved you so,
that he would never
wish a second marriage.
When all his folk
in court and land
pressed on him breathing
prayers and threats,
that he should help his country
and choose himself a consort;
when you yourself
urged on your king
the court's desire,
the country's wishes,
graciously be granted:
opposed to the court and land,
opposed to you yourself,
with tact and kindness
did he not decline,
till, Tristan, you did threaten
for ever to leave
the court and land,
if you yourself
were not dispatched

to woo for the king a bride?
He let it be that way.
This woman nonpareiled
your daring won for me,
who could behold her,
who could know her,
who so proudly
say he owned her
and not count himself most blessed?
Whom my will had
never dared to reach to,
whom my wish
feared to make a claim to,
whom, so nobly
good and gracious,
truly would
inspire my spirit;
'gainst foes and alarms,
a bride for a prince,
her you brought to me.
Now, when through such a
possession I
was more than before
aware of pain,
there where the wound
shows sore and open,
there have you struck me,
nevermore with
a hope to really recover,
why was I wounded
so terribly,
there, O most unblest one?
There with your poisoned
weapon so pierced,
that sense and brain
are scorched and burned,
destroying faith
in friend that was true,
and filling
frankest heart with distrust,
that I now covertly
dog my friend
by night, listening and spying,
bringing disrepute to my honor.
Why such hell to endure
which no heaven can save from?
Why this shameful blot
no suff'ring can atone?
That deep, inscrutable,
mysterious hidden cause—
who'll make it manifest?

TRISTAN
(*raising his eyes sympathizingly to Mark*)

O Sov'reign, I
cannot truly tell you;
and what you ask
can never have an answer.

*(Er wendet sich zu Isolde, die sehnsüchtig
zu ihm aufblickt.)*
Wohin nun Tristan scheidet,
willst du, Isold', ihm folgen?
Dem Land, das Tristan meint,
der Sonne Licht nicht scheint:
es ist das dunkel
nächt'ge Land,
daraus die Mutter
mich entsandt,
als, den im Tode
sie empfangen,
im Tod sie ließ
an das Licht gelangen.
Was, da sie mich gebar,
ihr Liebesberge war,
das Wunderreich der Nacht,
aus der ich einst erwacht:
das bietet dir Tristan,
dahin geht er voran:
ob sie ihm folge
treu und hold —
das sag ihm nun Isold'!

ISOLDE

Als für ein fremdes Land
der Freund sie einstens warb,
dem Unholden
treu und hold
mußt' Isolde folgen.
Nun führst du in Eigen,
dein Erbe mir zu zeigen;
wie flöh ich wohl das Land,
das alle Welt umspannt?
Wo Tristans Haus und Heim,
da kehr' Isolde ein:
auf dem sie folge
treu und hold,
den Weg nun zeig Isold'!
*(Tristan neigt sich langsam über sie und
küßt sie sanft auf die Stirn. — Melot fährt
wütend auf.)*

MELOT *(das Schwert ziehend)*

Verräter! Ha!
Zur Rache, König!
Duldest du diese Schmach?
*(Tristan zieht sein Schwert und wendet sich
schnell um.)*

TRISTAN

Wer wagt sein Leben an das meine?
(Er heftet den Blick auf Melot.)
Mein Freund war der,
er minnte mich hoch und teuer;
um Ehr' und Ruhm
mir war er besorgt wie keiner.

Zum Übermut
trieb er mein Herz;
die Schar führt' er,
die mich gedrängt,
Ehr' und Ruhm mir zu mehren,
dem König dich zu vermählen!
Dein Blick, Isolde,
blendet' auch ihn;
aus Eifer verriet
mich der Freund
dem König, den ich verriet!
(Er dringt auf Melot ein.)
Wehr dich, Melot!
*(Als Melot ihm das Schwert entgegenstreckt,
läßt Tristan das seinige fallen und sinkt verwundet in Kurwenals Arme. Isolde stürzt
sich an seine Brust. Marke hält Melot
zurück. Der Vorhang fällt schnell.)*

DRITTER AUFZUG

*Burggarten. Zur einen Seite hohe Burgge-
bäude, zur andren eine niedrige Mauerbrüstung, von einer Warte unterbrochen;
im Hintergrunde das Burgtor. Die Lage
ist auf felsiger Höhe anzunehmen; durch
Öffnungen blickt man auf einen weiten
Meereshorizont. Das Ganze macht den
Eindruck der Herrenlosigkeit, übel gepflegt, hie und da schadhaft und bewach-
sen.*

*Im Vordergrunde, an der inneren Seite,
liegt Tristan, unter dem Schatten einer
großen Linde, auf einem Ruhebett schla-
fend, wie leblos ausgestreckt. Zu Häup-
ten ihm sitzt Kurwenal, in Schmerz über
ihn hingebeugt und sorgsam seinem
Atem lauschend. Von der Außenseite her
hört man, beim Aufziehen des Vorhan-
ges, einen Hirtenreigen, sehnsüchtig und
traurig auf einer Schalmei geblasen. Endlich erscheint der Hirt selbst mit dem
Oberleibe über der Mauerbrüstung und
blickt teilnehmend herein.*

ERSTER AUFTRITT

HIRT

Kurwenal! He!
Sag, Kurwenal!
Hör doch, Freund!
*(Kurwenal wendet ein wenig das Haupt nach
ihm.)*

KURWENAL
(schüttelt traurig mit dem Kopf)

Erwachte er,
wär's doch nur,
um für immer zu verscheiden:

(He turns toward Isolde, who looks up longingly to him.)
Now whither Tristan travels,
will you, Isolde, follow?
The land that Tristan means
no sunlight can illume:
it is the dark
nocturnal land
from whence my mother
sent me forth
when, in the throes of
death they bore me;
in dying
she gave me to daylight's kingdom.
From the time I was born
her loving refuge was
the wonder-realm of night,
from where I woke to light.
Such Tristan offers you,
and first he goes before;
if she will follow,
kind and true,
let Isold' speak right now!

ISOLDE

Once, when a friend did
woo her for a foreign land,
the one kind and
gracious followed
the unkind master.
Now lead to your dominions,
your heritage to show me;
how should I flee that land
that spans the wide world round?
Where Tristan has his home
there will Isolde stay:
the way she follows,
kind and true,
that way now show Isold'!
Tristan bends slowly down to her and kisses her gently on her forehead. Melot starts angrily forward.

MELOT *(drawing his sword)*

You traitor! Ha!
My king, take vengeance!
Will you bear such a shame?

TRISTAN

Who dares to pit his life against mine?
(Fixing his gaze on Melot.)
My friend was he,
he loved me dearly and truly;
none cared so much
about my fame and my honor.

He made my heart
arrogant-proud;
he led forces
that urged me act,
make an increase to honor,
by wedding you to our monarch!
Your glance, Isolde,
dazzled him, too,
and passion then made
him betray
to the monarch, whom I betrayed!
(He sets on Melot.)
On guard, Melot!
(As Melot thrusts his sword at him, Tristan lets his fall and sinks wounded into Kurvenal's arms; Isolde throws herself upon his breast. Mark holds back Melot. The curtain falls quickly.)

ACT III

The garden of a castle. At one side are high turrets; on the other is a low breastwork broken by a watchtower; at back, the castle gate. The site is on rocky cliffs; through openings one looks over a wide sea to the horizon. The whole scene gives an impression of being ownerless, badly kept, here and there dilapidated and overgrown.

In the foreground inside lies Tristan sleeping on a couch, under the shade of a great lime tree. He is extended as if lifeless. At his head sits Kurvenal, bending over him in grief, and anxiously listening to his breathing. From without comes the sound of a shepherd's pipe. The upper half of the shepherd's body shows over the breastwork as he looks on sympathetically.

SCENE I

SHEPHERD

Kurvenal! Hey!
Say, Kurvenal!
Hear me, friend!
Has he not waked?
(Kurvenal turns his head a little toward him.)

KURVENAL
(shaking his head sadly)

Were he to wake,
it would be
just to part from us forever:

erschien zuvor
die Ärztin nicht,
die einz'ge, die uns hilft. —
Sahst du noch nichts?
Kein Schiff noch auf der See?

HIRT

Eine andre Weise
hörtest du dann,
so lustig, als ich sie nur kann.
Nun sag auch ehrlich,
alter Freund:
was hat's mit unserm Herrn?

KURWENAL

Laß die Frage:
du kannst's doch nie erfahren.
Eifrig späh,
und siehst du ein Schiff,
so spiele lustig und hell!
(Der Hirt wendet sich und späht, mit der
Hand überm Auge, nach dem Meer aus.)

HIRT

Öd und leer das Meer!
(Er setzt die Schalmei an den Mund und
entfernt sich blasend.)

TRISTAN (bewegungslos, dumpf)

Die alte Weise; —
Was weckt sie mich?

KURWENAL (fährt erschrocken auf)

Ha!

TRISTAN

Wo bin ich?

KURWENAL

Ha! Diese Stimme!
Seine Stimme!
Tristan! Herre!
Mein Held! Mein Tristan!

TRISTAN (mit Anstrengung)

Wer ruft mich?

KURWENAL

Endlich! Endlich!
Leben, o Leben!
Süßes Leben,
meinem Tristan neu gegeben!

TRISTAN (matt)

Kurwenal — du?
Wo war ich?
Wo bin ich?

KURWENAL

Wo du bist?
In Frieden, sicher und frei!
Kareol, Herr:
kennst du die Burg
der Väter nicht?

TRISTAN

Meiner Väter?

KURWENAL

Sieh dich nur um!

TRISTAN

Was erklang mir?

KURWENAL

Des Hirten Weise
hörtest du wieder;
am Hügel ab
hütet er deine Herde.

TRISTAN

Meine Herde?

KURWENAL

Herr, das mein' ich!
Dein das Haus,
Hof und Burg!
Das Volk, getreu
dem trauten Herrn,
so gut es konnt',
hat's Haus und Hof gepflegt,
das einst mein Held
zu Erb' und Eigen
an Leut' und Volk verschenkt,
als alles er verließ,
in fremde Land' zu ziehn.

TRISTAN

In welches Land?

KURWENAL

Hei! Nach Kornwall:
kühn und wonnig,
was sich da Glanzes,
Glückes und Ehren
Tristan, mein Held, hehr ertrotzt!

TRISTAN

Bin ich in Kornwall?

KURWENAL

Nicht doch: in Kareol!

TRISTAN

Wie kam ich her?

unless there comes
the one who heals,
for she alone can help.
What have you seen?
No ship yet on the sea?

SHEPHERD

I would play you quite a
different tune,
as merry a one as I could.
Now tell me rightly,
trusty friend:
how goes it with our lord?

KURVENAL

Leave that question:
you cannot learn by asking.
Scan the sea,
and if you see sails,
then pipe out blithely and clear!
(The shepherd turns round and scans the sea,
shading his eyes with his hand.)

SHEPHERD

Bleak and bare the sea!
(He puts the pipe to his mouth and with-
draws, playing.)

TRISTAN (without moving, faintly)

Why does it wake me—
that ancient tune?

KURVENAL (with a start of surprise)

Ha!

TRISTAN

Where am I?

KURVENAL

Now I hear him!
He is speaking!
Tristan! Master!
My lord! My hero!

TRISTAN (with effort)

Who calls me?

KURVENAL

Life! At last comes
life for my hero!
Life, sweet life, given
anew to bless my Tristan!

TRISTAN (feebly)

Kurvenal, you?
Where was I?
Where am I?

KURVENAL

Where are you?
In peace that's free and secure!
Kareol, lord:
do you not know
your father's halls?

TRISTAN

How? My father's?

KURVENAL

Just look around!

TRISTAN

What just sounded?

KURVENAL

Again you heard the
shepherd's tune sounding;
He tends your flocks
over there on the hillside.

TRISTAN

Are they my flocks?

KURVENAL

Sire, I say so!
Yours are house,
court, and fort!
The folk who truly
love their lord
as best they could
have kept the house and court
that once my hero
did bequeath to
his vassals and his serfs,
that time he left all here
to hie to foreign land.

TRISTAN

What foreign land?

KURVENAL

Why, to Cornwall:
where my Tristan,
brave and gallant,
proudly defiant,
won fortune, honors, and fame!

TRISTAN

Am I in Cornwall?

KURVENAL

Not now: in Kareol.

TRISTAN

How came I here?

KURWENAL

Hei nun! Wie du kamst?
Zu Roß rittest du nicht;
ein Schifflein führte dich her.
Doch zu dem Schifflein
hier auf den Schultern
trug ich dich; — die sind breit:
sie trugen dich dort zum Strand.
Nun bist du daheim, daheim zu Land:
im echten Land,
im Heimatland;
auf eigner Weid' und Wonne,
im Schein der alten Sonne,
darin von Tod und Wunden
du selig sollst gesunden.
(Er schmiegt sich an Tristans Brust.)

TRISTAN

Dünkt dich das?
Ich weiß es anders,
doch kann ich's dir nicht sagen.
Wo ich erwacht —
weilt' ich nicht;
doch, wo ich weilte,
das kann ich dir nicht sagen.
Die Sonne sah ich nicht,
noch sah ich Land und Leute:
doch, was ich sah,
das kann ich dir nicht sagen.
Ich war,
wo ich von je gewesen,
wohin auf je ich geh':
im weiten Reich
der Weltennacht.
Nur ein Wissen
dort uns eigen:
göttlich ew'ges
Ur-Vergessen!
Wie schwand mir seine Ahnung?
Sehnsücht'ge Mahnung,
nenn' ich dich,
die neu dem Licht
des Tags mich zugetrieben?
Was einzig mir geblieben;
ein heiß-inbrünstig Lieben,
aus Todes-Wonne-Grauen
jagt's mich, das Licht zu schauen,
das trügend hell und golden
noch dir, Isolden, scheint!
Isolde noch
im Reich der Sonne!
Im Tagesschimmer
noch Isolde!
Welches Sehnen!
Welches Bangen!
Sie zu sehen,
welch Verlangen!
Krachend hört' ich
hinter mir

schon des Todes
Tor sich schließen:
weit nun steht es
wieder offen,
der Sonne Strahlen
sprengt' es auf;
mit hell erschloßnen Augen
mußt' ich der Nacht enttauchen —
sie zu suchen,
sie zu sehen;
sie zu finden,
in der einzig
zu vergehen,
zu entschwinden
Tristan ist vergönnt.
Weh, nun wächst,
bleich und bang,
mir des Tages
wilder Drang;
grell und täuschend
sein Gestirn
weckt zu Trug
und Wahn mir das Hirn!
Verfluchter Tag
mit deinem Schein!
Wachst du ewig
meiner Pein?
Brennt sie ewig,
diese Leuchte,
die selbst nachts
von ihr mich scheuchte?
Ach, Isolde,
süße Holde!
Wann endlich,
wann, ach wann
löschest du die Zünde,
daß sie mein Glück mir künde?
Das Licht — wann löscht es aus?
(Er sinkt erschöpft leise zurück.)
Wann wird es Nacht im Haus?

KURWENAL

Der einst ich trotzt',
aus Treu' zu dir,
mit dir nach ihr
nun muß ich mich sehnen.
Glaub meinem Wort:
du sollst sie sehen
hier und heut;
den Trost kann ich dir geben —
ist sie nur selbst noch am Leben.

TRISTAN *(sehr matt)*

Noch losch das Licht nicht aus,
noch ward's nicht Nacht im Haus:
Isolde lebt und wacht;
sie rief mich aus der Nacht.

KURVENAL

Well, now! How you came?
You rode not on a horse;
a small ship carried you here:
I bore you on my
shoulders and brought you
to the boat;
they are broad:
they carried you to the shore.
Now you are at home, at home on land,
in your own land,
your native land;
among your happy pastures,
the old sun's rays will heal you;
from death and all your wounds you
shall blessedly recover.
(He clings to Tristan's breast.)

TRISTAN

Think you so?
I know it better,
and yet I cannot tell it.
I did not stay—
where I woke;
yet where I tarried,
I cannot really tell you.
The sun I did not see,
nor saw I land and people:
yet, what I saw,
I can indeed not tell you.
I was
where I have been forever,
where I forever go:
the realm of night
which girds the world.
We have there one knowledge only:
godlike, endless
prime oblivion!
How did foreknowledge vanish?
Yearning monition,
is it such,
that drives me back
into the realm of daylight?
All that survived within me,
a love ardent and burning,
that drives me forth from death's dread
rapture to look on daylight,
that falsely bright and golden,
still on you, Isolde, shines!
Isolde still in realms of sunlight!
The land of day still holds Isolde!
Ah, what longing!
What dread fretting!
What a yearning
now to see her!
Crashing sounds I've
heard already
when death's door

slammed behind me:
now again that
door stands open;
the streaming sunlight
burst it wide:
with clear, wide-open eyes I
must rise from out night's kingdom,
just to seek her,
just to see her,
just to find the
one in whom
alone I'll lose myself,
in whom alone
I cease to be.
Woe, now comes,
pale and fearful,
the wild distress of day;
dazzling speciously,
its eye
wakes my brain
to fraud and delusion!
Accursed day,
accursed glare!
Must you ever
wake my woe?
Must that beacon
burn forever,
making nights
a fear to see her?
Ah, Isolde,
sweet and gracious!
When, finally,
will you
quench the beacon signal,
that it announce my happiness?
The light, when will it die?
(He sinks back gently, exhausted.)
When will the house be still?

KURVENAL

Whom once I braved,
through faith in you,
I now do long
for, just the way you do.
Trust in my word:
I know you'll see her,
here, today:
that solace I can give you,
if only she still be living.

TRISTAN (very faintly)

The light is not yet out,
the house is still not dark:
Isolde lives and wakes;
she called me from the night.

KURWENAL

Lebt sie denn,
so laß dir Hoffnung lachen!
Muß Kurwenal dumm dir gelten,
heut sollst du ihn nicht schelten.
Wie tot lagst du
seit dem Tag,
da Melot, der Verruchte,
dir eine Wunde schlug.
Die böse Wunde,
wie sie heilen?
Mir tör'gem Manne
dünkt' es da,
wer einst dir Morolds
Wunde schloß,
der heilte leicht die Plagen
von Melots Wehr geschlagen.
Die beste Ärztin
bald ich fand;
nach Kornwall hab' ich
ausgesandt:
ein treuer Mann
wohl übers Meer
bringt dir Isolden her.

TRISTAN *(außer sich)*

Isolde kommt!
Isolde naht!
(Er ringt gleichsam nach Sprache.)
O Treue! Hehre,
holde Treue!
(Er zieht Kurwenal an sich und umarmt ihn.)
Mein Kurwenal,
du trauter Freund!
Du Treuer ohne Wanken,
wie soll dir Tristan danken?
Mein Schild, mein Schirm
in Kampf und Streit,
zu Lust und Leid
mir stets bereit:
wen ich gehaßt,
den haßtest du;
wen ich geminnt,
den minntest du.
Dem guten Marke,
dient' ich ihm hold,
wie warst du ihm treuer als Gold!
Mußt' ich verraten
den edlen Herrn,
wie betrogst du ihn da so gern!
Dir nicht eigen,
einzig mein,
mit leidest du,
wenn ich leide:
nur was ich leide,
das kannst du nicht leiden!
Dies furchtbare Sehnen,
das mich sehrt;
dies schmachtende Brennen,

das mich zehrt;
wollt' ich dir's nennen,
könntest du's kennen:
nicht hier würdest du weilen,
zur Warte müßtest du eilen —
mit allen Sinnen
sehnend von hinnen
nach dorten trachten und spähen,
wo ihre Segel sich blähen,
wo vor den Winden,
mich zu finden,
von der Liebe Drang befeuert,
Isolde zu mir steuert! —
Es naht! Es naht
mit mutiger Hast!
Sie weht, sie weht —
die Flagge am Mast.
Das Schiff! Das Schiff!
Dort streicht es am Riff!
Siehst du es nicht? *(Heftig.)*
Kurwenal, siehst du es nicht?
(Als Kurwenal, um Tristan nicht zu verlassen, zögert, und dieser in schweigender Spannung auf ihn blickt, ertönt, wie zu Anfang, näher, dann ferner, die klagende Weise des Hirten.)

KURWENAL *(niedergeschlagen)*

Noch ist kein Schiff zu sehn!

TRISTAN
(hat mit abnehmender Aufregung und gelauscht beginnt nun mit wachsender Schwermut)

Muß ich dich so verstehn,
du alte ernste Weise,
mit deiner Klage Klang?
Durch Abendwehen
drang sie bang,
als einst dem Kind
des Vaters Tod verkündet.
Durch Morgengrauen
bang und bänger,
als der Sohn
der Mutter Los vernahm.
Da er mich zeugt' und starb,
sie sterbend mich gebar.
Die alte Weise
sehnsuchtbang
zu ihnen wohl
auch klagend drang,
die einst mich frug
und jetzt mich frägt:
zu welchem Los erkoren,
ich damals wohl geboren?
Zu welchem Los?
Die alte Weise
sagt mir's wieder:

KURVENAL

If she lives,
then let this hope console you!
Though Kurvenal seem quite simple,
today you shall not blame him.
As dead I have
seen you lie
since Melot, the accursed,
dealt you a heavy wound.
This wound so grievous—
how to heal it?
I, foolish fellow,
had the thought
that she, who once healed
Morold's wounds,
could quickly heal the injury
that Melot's weapon dealt you.
I found the best
physician soon;
I've summoned her from
Cornwall's shores:
a trusty man
soon will arrive,
bringing Isolde here.

TRISTAN (transported)

Isolde comes!
Isold' draws nigh!
(He struggles to find words.)
O constancy!
Lofty, lovely loyalty!
(He draws Kurvenal toward him and embraces him.)
O Kurvenal,
my trusty friend!
Most loyal, never wav'ring,
how shall your Tristan thank you?
My shield, my fort
in war and strife,
one always there
through weal or woe:
whom I did hate,
you hated, too;
whom I have loved,
you loved, as well.
When truly serving
kindly King Mark,
you were to him truer than gold!
When I betrayed, though,
my noble lord,
how you gladly betrayed him too!
Yours you are not,
only mine;
you suffer too,
when I suffer;
that can you not suffer!
This terrible yearning
sears my soul;
this languishing burning

that consumes;
if I would tell it,
if you could know it:
no more here would you tarry,
you'd have to haste to the tower,
with all your senses
longingly straining
and seaward striving and watching,
where now her sails must be spreading,
and winds assisting,
where to find me;
fired by driving love's impatience,
Isold' is steering to me.
She comes, she comes,
with valorous haste!
It waves, it waves,
the flag on the masthead!
The ship! The ship!
It cleaves through the reef!
Do you not see?
Kurvenal! Do you not see?
(As Kurvenal hesitates to leave Tristan, who gazes at him in mute expectation, the mournful tune of the shepherd is heard, as at the beginning.)

KURVENAL (dejectedly)

Still there's no ship to see.

TRISTAN

(has listened with waning
excitement, and now begins to
speak with growing melancholy.)

Must I explain you thus,
you air so old and solemn,
with your so plaintive sound?
Through evening air your
sound was dread,
when once a child
was piped his father's passing;
through morning grayness,
still more fearful,
when the son
was told his mother's fate.
He died before my birth,
when I was born, she died;
the ancient song of
boding longing
gave wailing sounds
they must have heard;
it asked me once,
and asks me now:
What fate was I allotted,
the day my mother bore me?
What is my fate?
That strain so ancient
once more tells me:

mich sehnen — und sterben!
Nein! Ach nein!
So heißt sie nicht!
Sehnen! Sehnen!
Im Sterben mich zu sehnen,
vor Sehnsucht nicht zu sterben!
Die nie erstirbt,
sehnend nun ruft
um Sterbens Ruh
sie der fernen Ärztin zu. —
Sterbend lag ich
stumm im Kahn,
der Wunde Gift
dem Herzen nah:
Sehnsucht klagend
klang die Weise;
den Segel blähte der Wind
hin zu Irlands Kind.
Die Wunde, die
sie heilend schloß,
riß mit dem Schwert
sie wieder los;
das Schwert dann aber —
ließ sie sinken;
den Gifttrank gab sie
mir zu trinken:
wie ich da hoffte
ganz zu genesen,
da ward der sehrendste
Zauber erlesen:
daß nie ich sollte sterben,
mich ew'ger Qual vererben!
Der Trank! Der Trank!
Der furchtbare Trank!
Wie vom Herz zum Hirn
er wütend mir drang!
Kein Heil nun kann,
kein süßer Tod
je mich befrein
von der Sehnsucht Not;
nirgends, ach nirgends
find' ich Ruh:
mich wirft die Nacht
dem Tage zu,
um ewig an meinen Leiden
der Sonne Auge zu weiden.
O dieser Sonne
sengender Strahl,
wie brennt mir das Hirn
seine glühende Qual!
Für dieser Hitze
heißes Verschmachten,
ach, keines Schattens
kühlend Umnachten!
Für dieser Schmerzen
schreckliche Pein,
welcher Balsam sollte
mir Lindrung verleihn?
Den furchtbaren Trank,

der der Qual mich vertraut,
ich selbst — ich selbst,
ich hab' ihn gebraut!
Aus Vaters Not
und Mutterweh,
aus Liebestränen
eh und je —
aus Lachen und Weinen,
Wonnen und Wunden
hab' ich des Trankes
Gifte gefunden!
Den ich gebraut,
der mir geflossen,
den wonneschlürfend
je ich genossen —
verflucht sei, furchtbarer Trank!
Verflucht, wer dich gebraut!

KURWENAL
*(der vergebens Tristan zu mäßigen
suchte, schreit entsetzt auf)*

Mein Herre! Tristan!
Schrecklicher Zauber!
O Minnetrug!
O Liebeszwang!
Der Welt holdester Wahn,
wie ist's um dich getan!
Hier liegt er nun,
der wonnige Mann,
der wie keiner geliebt und geminnt.
Nun seht, was von ihm
sie Dankes gewann,
was je Minne sich gewinnt!
(Mit schluchzender Stimme.)
Bist du nun tot?
Lebst du noch?
Hat dich der Fluch entführt?
(Er lauscht seinem Atem.)
O Wonne! Nein!
Er regt sich, er lebt!
Wie sanft er die Lippen rührt!

TRISTAN
(langsam wieder zu sich kommend)
Das Schiff? Siehst du's noch nicht?

KURWENAL

Das Schiff? Gewiß,
es naht noch heut;
es kann nicht lang mehr säumen.

TRISTAN

Und drauf Isolde,
wie sie winkt —
wie sie hold
mir Sühne trinkt.
Siehst du sie?
Siehst du sie noch nicht?

of yearning and dying!
No! Ah, no!
It bids not that!
Yearning! Yearning!
In dying I must yearn on,
but must not die of yearning.
What never dies,
yearningly calls
the distant healer
and asks for death's repose.
Dying, I lay
mute on deck,
the poisoned wound
was near my heart:
drear the song, and
melancholy;
the breezes filling the sails
urged to Ireland's child.
The wound her healing
hand had closed
she opened once
more with her sword,
the sword then—after—
she relinquished;
the poisoned potion
that she gave me,
I hoped it would
completely restore me;
its searing magic, though,
had for intention
that death should never find me,
but endless torment take me!
The drink!
The drink, the terrible drink!
How from heart to head
it filled me with fire!
No healing art,
nor kindly death
can make me free
from this yearning need.
Nowhere, ah, nowhere
find I rest;
I'm cast by night
into the day,
where sun's gloating eye is ever
the witness to all my sorrow.
Oh, how the scorching
glare of the sun
does blister my brain
with its torturing glow!
Against this heat that
withers and parches,
there comes no help from
night's cooling darkness.
Against this great and
terrible pain,
where's balsam that can
bring healing relief?
The horrible drink

with the torment it gave—
myself, myself
caused it to be brewed!
My father's grief
and mother's woe,
the tears of love
to come, and past,
the laughing and weeping,
joying and wounding—
these did I make a
poisonous potion.
What was then brewed,
what I had taken,
that ever gave me
joy in the sipping.
I curse you, terrible drink!
Accursed who made your brew!

KURVENAL

*(who has been vainly striving to calm
Tristan, cries out in terror)*

Frightful enchantment!
Oh, love's deceit!
Oh, passion's pow'r!
The world's loveliest dream!
What is this you have done!
here lies he now,
the rarest of men,
no one like him so loved and adored!
Behold, what return
his love has obtained,
which is all love ever wins.
(His voice broken by sobs.)
Are you now dead?
Do you live?
Have you fulfilled the curse?
(He listens for his breath.)
O rapture! No!
He's stirring! He lives!
How gently he moves his lips!

TRISTAN
(beginning very faintly)

The ship? Is it in sight?

KURVENAL

The ship? Indeed,
it comes today:
it can't delay much longer.

TRISTAN

On board, Isolde,
how she waves,
how she sweetly
drinks our peace:
Do you see?
Can't you see her yet?

Wie sie selig,
hehr und milde
wandelt durch
des Meers Gefilde?
Auf wonniger Blumen
lichten Wogen
kommt sie sanft
ans Land gezogen.
Sie lächelt mir Trost
und süße Ruh,
sie führt mir letzte
Labung zu.
Ach, Isolde! Isolde!
Wie schön bist du!
Und Kurwenal, wie,
du sähst sie nicht?
Hinauf zur Warte,
du blöder Wicht!
Was so hell und licht ich sehe,
daß das dir nicht entgehe!
Hörst du mich nicht?
Zur Warte schnell!
Eilig zur Warte!
Bist du zur Stell'?
Das Schiff? Das Schiff?
Isoldens Schiff?
Du mußt es sehen!
Mußt es sehen!
Das Schiff? Sähst du's noch nicht?
(Während Kurwenal noch zögernd mit Tris-
tan ringt, läßt der Hirt von außen die Schal-
mei ertönen. Kurwenal springt freudig auf.)

KURWENAL

O Wonne! Freude!
(Er stürzt auf die Warte und späht aus.)
Ha! Das Schiff!
Von Norden seh' ich's nahen.

TRISTAN

Wußt' ich's nicht?
Sagt' ich's nicht,
daß sie noch lebt,
noch Leben mir webt?
Die mir Isolde
einzig enthält,
wie wär' Isolde
mir aus der Welt?

KURWENAL
(von der Warte zurückrufend, jauchzend)

Heiha! Heiha!
Wie es mutig steuert!
Wie stark der Segel sich bläht!
Wie es jagt, wie es fliegt!

TRISTAN

Die Flagge? Die Flagge?

KURWENAL

Der Freude Flagge
am Wimpel lustig und hell!

TRISTAN
(auf dem Lager hoch sich aufrichtend)

Hahei! Der Freude!
Hell am Tage
zu mir Isolde!
Isolde zu mir!
Siehst du sie selbst?

KURWENAL

Jetzt schwand das Schiff
hinter dem Fels.

TRISTAN

Hinter dem Riff?
Bringt es Gefahr?
Dort wütet die Brandung,
scheitern die Schiffe!
Das Steuer, wer führt's?

KURWENAL

Der sicherste Seemann.

TRISTAN

Verriet' er mich?
Wär' er Melots Genoß?

KURWENAL

Trau ihm wie mir!

TRISTAN

Verräter auch du!
Unsel'ger!
Siehst du sie wieder?

KURWENAL

Noch nicht.

TRISTAN

Verloren!

KURWENAL *(jauchzend)*

Heiha! Hei ha ha ha ha!
Vorbei! Vorbei!
Glücklich vorbei!

TRISTAN

Kurwenal, hei ha ha ha!
treuester Freund!
All mein Hab und Gut
vererb' ich noch heute.

KURWENAL

Sie nahen im Flug.

How she, blest and
mild and noble,
makes her way
through sea's expanses?
On luminous waves of
lovely flowers,
see her draw
to gentle landing.
Her smile brings me peace
and sweet repose,
she gives me
uttermost relief.
Ah, Isolde! Isolde!
How fair you are!
And Kurvenal, how,
you saw her not?
Go up the watchtow'r,
you purblind wretch!
What I saw so bright and clearly
make sure it not escapes you.
Do you not hear?
The watchtow'r, quick!
Haste to the watchtow'r!
Are you still here?
The ship? The ship?
Isolde's ship!
You have to see it!
You must see it!
The ship? Don't you see it?
(Whilst Kurvenal, still hesitating, opposes
Tristan, the shepherd's merry piping is heard
without.)

KURVENAL

O rapture! Marv'lous!
(He rushes to the watchtower and looks out.)
Ha! The ship!
From northward it is coming.

TRISTAN

Did I know?
Was I right?
That she still lives,
still knits me to life.
For me the world
contains only Isolde,
how then could
she leave the world!

KURVENAL *(shouting)*

Ahoy! Ahoy!
See it bravely tacking!
The sail is full with the wind!
How it drives, how it plies!

TRISTAN

The pennant! The pennant!

KURVENAL

The joyful pennant
at topmast, merry and bright!

TRISTAN
(raising himself up from his couch)

Ahoy, what rapture!
Bright the day
that has brought Isolde!
Isolde comes here!
D'you see her there?

KURVENAL

It went, just now,
hid by the rock.

TRISTAN

Hid by the reef?
Is there some risk?
There breakers are raging,
vessels have foundered!
Who stands at the helm?

KURVENAL

The surest of seamen.

TRISTAN

Has he betrayed?
Could he be Melot's friend?

KURVENAL

Trust him like me!

TRISTAN

A traitor like you!
Unblest one!
Has it come back yet?

KURVENAL

Not yet.

TRISTAN

It's done for!

KURVENAL *(shouting)*

Ahoy, ahoy, ahoy!
They're past, they're through,
safely, they're through!

TRISTAN

Ahoy, ahoy! Kurvenal,
truest of friends!
All my worldly goods
today I bequeath you.

KURVENAL

They're coming full speed!

TRISTAN

Siehst du sie endlich?
Siehst du Isolde?

KURWENAL

Sie ist's! Sie winkt!

TRISTAN

O seligstes Weib!

KURWENAL

Im Hafen der Kiel!
Isolde, ha!
Mit einem Sprung
springt sie vom Bord ans Land.

TRISTAN

Herab von der Warte,
müßiger Gaffer!
Hinab! Hinab
an den Strand!
Hilf ihr! Hilf meiner Frau!

KURWENAL

Sie trag' ich herauf:
trau meinen Armen!
Doch du, Tristan,
bleib mir treulich am Bett.
(Kurwenal eilt fort.)

ZWEITER AUFTRITT

TRISTAN
*(in höchster Aufregung
auf dem Lager sich mühend)*

O diese Sonne!
Ha, dieser Tag!
Ha, dieser Wonne
sonnigster Tag!
Jagendes Blut,
jauchzender Mut!
Lust ohne Maßen,
freudiges Rasen!
Auf des Lagers Bann
wie sie ertragen!
Wohlauf und daran,
wo die Herzen schlagen!
Tristan der Held,
in jubelnder Kraft,
hat sich vom Tod
emporgerafft!
(Er richtet sich hoch auf.)
Mit blutender Wunde
bekämpft' ich einst Morolden,
mit blutender Wunde
erjag' ich mir heut Isolden!

(Er reißt sich den Verband der Wunde auf.)
Heia, mein Blut!
Lustig nun fließe!
*(Er springt vom Lager herab und schwankt
vorwärts.)*
Die mir die Wunde
auf ewig schließe —
sie naht wie ein Held,
sie naht mir zum Heil!
Vergeh' die Welt
meiner jauchzenden Eil'!
(Er taumelt nach der Mitte der Bühne.)

ISOLDE *(von außen)*

Tristan! Geliebter!

TRISTAN
(in der furchtbarsten Aufregung)

Wie, hör' ich das Licht?
Die Leuchte, ha!
Die Leuchte verlischt!
Zu ihr! Zu ihr!
*(Isolde eilt atemlos herein. Tristan, seiner
nicht mächtig, stürzt sich ihr schwankend
entgegen. In der Mitte der Bühne begegnen
sie sich; sie empfängt ihn in ihren Armen.
Tristan sinkt langsam in ihren Armen zu
Boden.)*

ISOLDE

Tristan! Ha!

TRISTAN
(sterbend zu ihr aufblickend)

Isolde!
(Er stirbt.)

ISOLDE

Ha! Ich bin's, ich bin's,
süßester Freund!
Auf, noch einmal
hör meinen Ruf!
Isolde ruft:
Isolde kam,
mit Tristan treu zu sterben.
Bleibst du mir stumm?
Nur eine Stunde,
nur eine Stunde
bleibe mir wach!
So bange Tage
wachte sie sehnend,
um eine Stunde
mit dir noch zu wachen:
betrügt Isolden,
betrügt sie Tristan
um dieses einzige,
ewig kurze
letzte Weltenglück?

TRISTAN

Now can you see her?

KURVENAL

It's she! She waves!

TRISTAN

O woman most blest!

KURVENAL

The vessel is home!
Isolde, ha!
a single spring
brings her from deck to land.

TRISTAN

Get down from the watchtow'r,
indolent gaper!
Get down! Get down
to the shore!
Help her! Help my beloved!

KURVENAL

I'll bring her up here:
trust I can do it!
But you, Tristan,
stay right there on your couch.
(*Kurvenal hastens away.*)

SCENE II

TRISTAN
(*tossing on his couch
in extreme excitement*)

O blessed sunlight!
Ha, what a day!
Ha, what a joyful,
radiant day!
Tumult of blood,
jubilant pow'r!
Measureless pleasure!
Joyful delirium!
When confined to bed
how can I bear them?
Well, up then and off
to where hearts are beating!
Tristan, the knight,
in jubilant strength,
has dragged himself
away from death!
(*He raises himself quite up.*)
My wound was all bleeding
when once I fought with Morold:
so, bleeding it shall be
in struggling to have Isolde!

(*He tears the bandage from his wound.*)
Aha, my blood!
flow now, exulting!
(*He springs from his bed and staggers forward.*)
She who can close my
wound forever
most valiantly comes,
she comes for my good!
let earth now pass
in my jubilant haste!
(*He totters to the center of the stage.*)

ISOLDE (*without*)

Tristan! Beloved!

TRISTAN
(*in frantic excitement*)

Can I hear the light?
The torchlight, ha!
The torchlight is quenched!
To her! To her!
(*Isolde hastens breathlessly in. Tristan, out of
his senses, staggers weakly toward her. They
meet in the center of the stage; she receives
him in her arms. Tristan sinks slowly to the
ground in Isolde's arms.*)

ISOLDE

Tristan! Ha!

TRISTAN
(*raising his eyes to Isolde*)

Isolde!
(*He dies.*)

ISOLDE

Ha!
It's I, it's I,
sweetest of friends!
Up, this once more
hear when I call!
Isolde calls:
Isolde's here
to loy'lly die with Tristan!
Will you not speak?
Only an hour,
only an hour
stay awake, love!
I've spent such days in
anxiously yearning,
that I might wake with
you for one short hour.
Will you deceive me,
deceive Isolde
of even this single,
swiftly fleeting,
final earthly joy?

Die Wunde? Wo?
Laß sie mich heilen!
Daß wonnig und hehr
die Nacht wir teilen;
nicht an der Wunde,
an der Wunde stirb mir nicht:
uns beiden vereint
erlösche das Lebenslicht!
Gebrochen der Blick!
Still das Herz!
Nicht eines Atems
flücht'ges Wehn! —
Muß sie nun jammernd
vor dir stehn,
die sich wonnig dir zu vermählen
mutig kam übers Meer?
Zu spät!
Trotziger Mann!
Strafst du mich so
mit härtestem Bann?
Ganz ohne Huld
meiner Leidens-Schuld?
Nicht meine Klagen
darf ich dir sagen?
Nur einmal, ach!
nur einmal noch! —
Tristan! — Ha! —
Horch! Er wacht!
Geliebter!
(Sie sinkt bewußtlos über der Leiche zusammen.)

DRITTER AUFTRITT

Kurwenal war sogleich hinter Isolde zurückgekommen; sprachlos in furchtbarer Erschütterung hat er dem Auftritte beigewohnt und bewegungslos auf Tristan hingestarrt. Aus der Tiefe hört man jetzt dumpfes Gemurmel und Waffengeklirr. Der Hirt kommt über die Mauer gestiegen.

HIRT

Kurwenal! Hör!
Ein zweites Schiff.
(Kurwenal fährt heftig auf und blickt über die Brüstung, während der Hirt aus der Ferne erschüttert auf Tristan und Isolde sieht.)

KURWENAL

Tod und Hölle!
Alles zur Hand!
Marke und Melot
hab' ich erkannt.
Waffen und Steine!
Hilf mir! Ans Tor!
(Er eilt mit dem Hirten an das Tor, das sie in der Hast zu verrammeln suchen.)

DER STEUERMANN *(stürzt herein)*

Marke mir nach
mit Mann und Volk:
vergebne Wehr!
Bewältigt sind wir.

KURWENAL

Stell dich und hilf!
Solang ich lebe,
lugt mir keiner herein!

BRANGÄNES STIMME
(außen, von unten her)

Isolde! Herrin!

KURWENAL

Brangänens Ruf?
(Hinabrufend.)
Was suchst du hier?

BRANGÄNE

Schließ nicht, Kurwenal!
Wo ist Isolde?

KURWENAL

Verrät'rin auch du?
Weh dir, Verruchte!

MELOT *(außerhalb)*

Zurück, du Tor!
Stemm dich nicht dort!

KURWENAL *(wütend auflachend)*

Heiahaha! Dem Tag,
an dem ich dich treffe!
(Melot, mit gewaffneten Männern, erscheint unter dem Tor, Kurwenal stürzt sich auf ihn und streckt ihn zu Boden.)

KURWENAL

Stirb, schändlicher Wicht!

MELOT

Weh mir, Tristan!
(Er stirbt.)

BRANGÄNE *(noch außerhalb)*

Kurwenal! Wütender!
Hör, du betrügst dich!

KURWENAL

Treulose Magd!
(Zu den Seinen.)
Drauf! Mir nach!
Werft sie zurück!
(Sie kämpfen.)

The wound is where?
Oh, let me heal it,
that, raptured, we share
the night together!
Oh, do not perish
of your wound, oh, do not die:
let us both together
made one, lose the light of life!
How lifeless his glance!
Still—his heart!
No fleeting flutter
of his breath?
Must she stand mourning
by your side
who, so joyous, came here to wed you,
bravely sailing the sea?
Too late!
Obstinate man!
Why must my punishment
be so hard?
Is there no grace
for my sorrow's debt?
May I not tell you
what my complaints are?
Just once more, ah!
Just one more time!
Tristan! Ha!
Hark! He wakes!
Beloved!
(She sinks down senseless upon his body.)

SCENE III

*Kurvenal had entered immediately after
Isolde; in speechless horror, he has remained near the entrance, gazing motionless on Tristan. From below is now
heard the dull tumult of voices and clash
of weapons. The shepherd climbs over
the wall, then comes quickly and softly
to Kurvenal.*

SHEPHERD

Kurvenal! Hear!
A second ship!
*(Kurvenal starts up in haste and looks over
the rampart, while the shepherd stands apart,
gazing in consternation on Tristan and
Isolde.)*

KURVENAL

Death and hell-fire!
All of you, now!
Melot and Mark
I think I have seen!
Weapons and stones too!
Help me! To the gate!
*(He hurries with the shepherd to the gate,
which they hastily try to barricade.)*

THE STEERSMAN *(rushes in)*

Mark is behind
with men-at-arms:
defense is vain,
we're overpowered.

KURVENAL

Stand here and help!
While I am living
none can pry into here!

BRANGAENE
(without, calling from below)

Isolde! Mistress!

KURVENAL

Brangaene's voice!
(Calling down.)
What do you seek?

BRANGAENE

Don't close, Kurvenal!
Where is Isolde?

KURVENAL

A traitor, you too?
Woe to you, rascal!

MELOT *(without)*

Stand back, you fool!
Bar not the way!

KURVENAL *(laughing savagely)*

Hi-a-ha-ha! The day
has come I can strike you!
*(Melot with armed men appears under the
gateway. Kurvenal rushes upon him and
strikes him down.)*

KURVENAL

Die, villainous wretch!

MELOT

Woe's me! Tristan!
(He dies.)

BRANGAENE *(still without)*

Kurvenal! Do not
deceive yourself, madman!

KURVENAL

Treacherous maid!
(To his followers.)
Come! Follow!
Hurl them right back!
(They fight.)

MARKE *(außerhalb)*

Halte, Rasender!
Bist du von Sinnen?

KURWENAL

Hier wütet der Tod!
Nichts andres, König,
ist hier zu holen:
willst du ihn kiesen, so komm!
*(Er dringt auf Marke und dessen Gefolge
ein.)*

MARKE
(unter dem Tor mit Gefolge erscheinend)

Zurück! Wahnsinniger!

BRANGÄNE
*(hat sich seitwärts über die Mauer
geschwungen und eilt in den Vordergrund)*

Isolde! Herrin!
Glück und Heil!
Was seh' ich? Ha!
Lebst du? Isolde!
*(Sie müht sich um Isolde. — Marke mit
seinem Gefolge hat Kurwenal mit dessen
Helfern vom Tore zurückgetrieben und
dringt herein.)*

MARKE

O Trug und Wahn!
Tristan! Wo bist du?

KURWENAL
*(schwer verwundet, schwankt vor Marke
her nach dem Vordergrund)*

Da liegt er —
hier — wo ich — liege.
(Er sinkt bei Tristans Füßen zusammen.)

MARKE

Tristan! Tristan!
Isolde! Weh!

KURWENAL
(nach Tristans Hand fassend)

Tristan! Trauter!
Schilt mich nicht,
daß der Treue auch mit kommt!
(Er stirbt.)

MARKE

Tot denn alles!
Alles tot!
Mein Held, mein Tristan!
Trautester Freund,
auch heute noch
mußt du den Freund verraten?

Heut, wo er kommt,
dir höchste Treu' zu bewähren?
Erwache! Erwache!
Erwache meinem Jammer!
*(Schluchzend über die Leiche sich herab-
beugend.)*
Du treulos treuster Freund!

BRANGÄNE
*(die in ihren Armen Isolde
wieder zu sich gebracht)*

Sie wacht! Sie lebt!
Isolde! Hör mich,
vernimm meine Sühne!
Des Trankes Geheimnis
entdeckt' ich dem König:
mit sorgender Eil'
stach er in See,
dich zu erreichen,
dir zu entsagen,
dir zuzuführen den Freund.

MARKE

Warum, Isolde,
warum mir das?
Da hell mir enthüllt,
was zuvor ich nicht fassen konnt',
wie selig, daß den Freund
ich frei von Schuld da fand!
Dem holden Mann
dich zu vermählen,
mit vollen Segeln
flog ich dir nach.
Doch Unglückes
Ungestüm,
wie erreicht es, wer Frieden bringt?
Die Ernte mehrt' ich dem Tod,
der Wahn häufte die Not.

BRANGÄNE

Hörst du uns nicht?
Isolde! Traute!
Vernimmst du die Treue nicht?
*(Isolde, die nichts um sich her vernommen,
heftet das Auge mit wachsender Begeister-
ung auf Tristans Leiche.)*

ISOLDE

Mild und leise
wie er lächelt,
wie das Auge
hold er öffnet —
seht ihr's, Freunde?
Seht ihr's nicht?
Immer lichter
wie er leuchtet,
stern-umstrahlet
hoch sich hebt?

MARK *(half in)*

Halt, you blusterer!
Are you demented?

KURVENAL

Here rages but death!
There's nothing, King,
besides to be had here:
if you would choose it, then come!
(He sets upon Mark and his followers.)

MARK
(appearing under the gate with his men)

Go back, you maniac!

BRANGAENE
*(has climbed over the wall at the
side and hastens to the front.)*

Isolde! Mistress!
Joyful news!
What sight's this? Ha!
Are you still living?
*(She devotes herself to Isolde. Mark with
his followers has driven Kurvenal and his
assistants back from the gate and forced his
way in)*

MARK

Oh, dread mistake!
Tristan! Where are you?

KURVENAL
*(mortally wounded, totters before
Mark toward the front.)*

There lies he—
here—where I—lie too!
(He sinks down at Tristan's feet.)

MARK

Tristan! Tristan!
Isolde! Woe!

KURVENAL
(clutching at Tristan's hand)

Tristan! Master!
Blame me not
who, all faithful, join you now!
(He dies.)

MARK

All are dead, then!
All are dead!
My hero, Tristan!
Truest of friends,
so even on
this day you must betray me?

Just when he comes
to prove his perfect trust in Tristan?
Awaken! Awaken!
Awaken to my sorrow!
(Bending down sobbing over the bodies.)
You faithless, faithful friend!

BRANGAENE
(who has revived Isolde in her arms)

She wakes! She lives!
Isolde, hear me!
Oh, hear my atonement!
The king knows the secret:
I told of the potion.
He sped over sea,
greatly concerned
that he might reach you,
just to renounce you
and make you one with your friend!

MARK

Oh, why, Isolde,
why this to me?
When that was revealed
which before I had failed to grasp,
how blessed that I found
my friend was free from guilt!
That you might wed
hero so gallant,
with outspread sails
I flew in your wake.
Yet how can one bringing peace
get the better of raging woe!
I swelled the harvest of death;
Vain dreams only heap woe!

BRANGAENE

Do you not hear?
Isolde! Dearest!
Oh, look on your faithful maid!
*(Isolde, unconscious of all around her, turn-
ing her eyes on Tristan's body with rising
inspiration.)*

ISOLDE

See him smiling,
softly, gently,
see the eyes that
open fondly,
O my friends here,
don't you 'see?
Ever lighter
how he's shining,
borne on high
amid the stars?

Seht ihr's nicht?
Wie das Herz ihm
mutig schwillt,
voll und hehr
im Busen ihm quillt?
Wie den Lippen,
wonnig mild,
süßer Atem
sanft entweht —
Freunde! Seht!
Fühlt und seht ihr's nicht?
Hör' ich nur
diese Weise,
die so wunder-
voll und leise,
Wonne klagend,
alles sagend,
mild versöhnend
aus ihm tönend,
in mich dringet,
auf sich schwinget,
hold erhallend
um mich klinget?
Heller schallend,
mich umwallend,

sind es Wellen
sanfter Lüfte?
Sind es Wogen
wonniger Düfte?
Wie sie schwellen,
mich umrauschen,
soll ich atmen,
soll ich lauschen?
Soll ich schlürfen,
untertauchen?
Süß in Düften
mich verhauchen?
In dem wogenden Schwall,
in dem tönenden Schall,
in des Welt-Atems
wehendem All —
ertrinken,
versinken —
unbewußt —
höchste Lust!

(Isolde sinkt, wie verklärt, in Brangänes Armen sanft auf Tristans Leiche. Große Rührung und Entrücktheit unter den Umstehenden. Marke segnet die Leichen. Der Vorhang fällt langsam.)

Don't you see?
How his heart so
bravely swells,
full and calm
it throbs in his breast!
How from lips so
joyful-mild
sweet the breath that
softly stirs—
Friends! See!
Don't you feel and see?
Is it only
I who hear these
gentle, wondrous
strains of music,
joyously sounding,
telling all things,
reconciling,
sounding from him,
piercing through me,
rising upward,
echoes fondly
round me ringing?
Ever clearer,
wafting round me,

are they waves of
gentle breezes?
Are they clouds of
gladdening perfumes?
As they swell and
murmur round me,
shall I breathe them,
shall I listen?
Shall I sip them,
plunge beneath them,
breathe my last
amid their fragrance?
In the billowy surge,
in the ocean of sound,
in the World Spirit's
infinite All,
to drown now,
descending,
void of thought—
highest bliss!

(Isolde sinks, as if transfigured, in Brangaene's arms upon Tristan's body. Profound emotion and grief of the bystanders. Mark invokes a blessing on the dead.)

CURTAIN